Scotland and Aye

Sophia Wasiak Butler

London | New York

Published by Clink Street Publishing 2019

First edition.

978-1-912562-07-7 paperback
978-1-912562-08-4 ebook

I dedicate this book to my Mum and Dad, for never ever giving up.

Acknowledgements

A London girl falls in love with a Scotsman and moves to a remote hamlet in Scotland.

These articles came out of the cultural shock of living in a rural place forgotten by time. Writing became my most faithful, dependable and nonjudgemental companion together with cigarettes and cheap wine.

The Polish newspaper in London 'Nowy Czas', decided to publish my musings on the experience and gave me a permanent presence in it's pages. The multicultural theme, very much in vogue at the time and ever present in the media opened the door for my type of writing.

I got immediate feed back from a varied readership. The repeating phrases for my 'adventures' were: "Bridget Jones goes rural in Scotland," "From party girl to country bumpkin in a couple of months." My misfortunes seemed to strike a chord with my readers. After all, everybody loved watching Bridget Jones fall flat on her face in a mudd puddle! I was a fish out of water, but even that was the understatement of the century!

Humour aside, my heart was on the line. I was in love, but in foreign waters and insecure on all fronts. My readers' emotional reaction to my story was seriously overwhelming, some people were willing to come and help start my garden, some gave practical advice on how to handle animals, and later in the story, I even got a marriage proposal to get me away from that 'brute' Scotsman!

They say, if God loves you, he'll grant you your wish. So I got the man of my dreams (then) and I got eco, self-sustainable country life. I did everything I could with the resources I had at the time. My deepest desire is that no-one should be stopped in following their heart and taking a chance. Each journey is unique and yes, it hurts, to realise that yours itsn't the one paved with roses. There is no shame in learning, in trying and those who tell you otherwise have probably never taken a chance in their lives. The likelihood is that their dreams are far more troubling than yours.

My gratitude goes to life itself because it is the source of everything. To all the people who crossed my path, because nobody is ever the sole creator of themselves. I thank my editors at 'Nowy Czas' for taking a chance on me. As for my readers, I'm holding them fully responsible for the enthusiastic encouragement which kept me going. My gratitude also goes to the Polonia Aid Foundation Trust for believing in me and for their support. I am very grateful to Frank Taylor for the gift of some of his photos to liven up these pages. A heartfelt thank-you to Curro Marcos for his unwaivering support, patience and endless supply of delicious tortillas and guitar music without which I could not have completed the book! Thank you to my wonderful Auntie Regina who would never stop reminding me :"Sophie, live cleverly, so you'll always find time for love and writing". I want to say the biggest thank you to my friends, whose contribution to my life is priceless and who know me like nobody else knows me. And finally, I would like to bow to my wonderful parents, my dad who put me on the path to spiritual growth and my mum, who embodies life's grace and beauty. My first and most vital teachers.

Have fun on the journey. I'll see you at the other end.

Sophia Wasiak Butler.

Before the Beginning

Trip on the River (Spływ Dunajcem)

If it's true that we only have two choices in life: what we do and who we do it with, I didn't know what I wanted to do and had nobody to do it with. As a literature graduate, I felt like a soldier in the Foreign Legion ready for hire. We were the generation of over-educated losers, because we lost out on the times when the economy was thriving, money was easy to make, jobs were plentiful and love was an easily obtainable commodity. My friends and I threw ourselves into revelling over the summer, anticipating the beginning of 'real' life. Those who chose more practical degrees found their three-year stint qualified them to do *something* – literature proved that I could read and write coherently and structure an opinion of a text – not skills which appear in an employer's top ten which seems to read 'Experience x10'. I was at a loss, my friends were either bogged down in further academia and the mire of a life-consuming Masters degree, or working jobs which made them want to 'end-it-all'. By chance a friend told me about the programme at the Uniwersytet Jagiellonski (Jagiellonian University): a six month to one-year course in the Polish language with a choice of subjects from cooking to Polish history. I knew I had to go, Kraków is my favourite city, far outweighing Venice or Paris in my humble opinion. It is truly romantic with its cobbled streets steeped in history, enchanting tiny alleyways and dungeon-like stone basements.

I have always felt a sense of being torn between two cultures and names: Sophia and Zosia. As a child I grew up in what we affectionately termed the 'United Nations': of all my inner city friends, not *one* was completely English, so the whole business of being picked up by relations and prszyszywane Ciocie[1] who did not speak English was an ordinary experience. I much preferred the freedom of Poland, spending every holiday there with my Ciocia and Wujek[2] who live in a small town. Each day I was let out to run free with all the children on the street, knowing I had to come back for obiad[3] at

1 People who you call Auntie but you have no actual blood relation to

2 Aunt and Uncle

3 Lunch

two o'clock and kolacja[4] followed by 'Dobranocka'[5] at seven. It was so much more relaxed than the London way of mums ringing each other and driving to surgically accurate playdates, until a quarter past four and not a minute more.

The freedom of expressing myself in two languages has been a discovery – I am completely different in each language and culture, but my identification had been primarily with Poland. Whether that is because my mother is Polish and I grew up with her, I am not sure. Yet, I felt that I had not completely immersed myself in 'Polishness' because I had never lived there. As I progressed through my okres buntu[6], I was able to stop fighting being English and accept that I am mixed, which allows me the possibility of picking the best qualities from each culture. It took me a long time to realise that in rejecting being English, I was rejecting half of myself, not to mention my father. Over time, having reconciled myself to being a 'mongrel' and embracing Britishness, I felt that I would like to live in Poland in order to meet the practicalities of being a citizen, such as the procedure for paying bills and opening a bank account. This opportunity was perfect. I trusted that I would have a wonderful six months because the city itself promotes contentedness in its beauty, but I could not have known that I would meet friends who I hope to know for the rest of my life.

At the Uniwersytet Jagiellonski we were told to walk around Kraków looking up and down from the kamiennice[7] to the dachy[8] in order to appreciate the richness of the city. Whilst there I met many mieszanki[9] like myself of all shapes and ages, with Polish heritage. There were students from Egypt, America, Australia and all over Europe. It was wonderful to interact with so many

4 Dinner

5 A goodnight story religiously watched by all Polish children after dinner and before bed

6 Rebellious period

7 Stone basements

8 Rooves

9 People with mixed cultural origins

'mixed' people who could all relate to the stereotypical bossy Polish mother and the Ciocie who kept you well fed over the holidays. Attending our school there were also a couple of men who had married Polish women and wished to learn the language (this greatly impressed everyone) and more than a few Japanese students who wished to be able to read Polish pedagogues who were not often translated into Japanese. One character who I remember with a smile, was a sixty-something retired Japanese man who was dismayed to find that his wife did not take to suddenly having him around the house with nothing to do. He therefore went to a language school, in pursuit of a hobby and the first teacher he had the opportunity to speak to, being a Polish one, sent him to Kraków where he was happily studying whilst living with a family.

The six months that I spent there were golden; full of pierogi ruskie[10], piwko[11], friends, dancing and walks by the Wisla. Nasza paczka[12] consisted of four girls: Detta from Australia, Ania from Germany but living in Italy, Basia from Hungary and of course myself from England. The two boys were Mateusz from America and Stefan from Holland. Together we were 'The Snobs' (ironically named because we had tried to encourage others to party with us and break-up language and ability groups, but without success). We were all on different language levels; some had been forced into Polish Sunday school, some had two parents at home speaking Polish and some had spent many holidays in the native land. The school provided classes for people from 'Dziendobry!'[13] to Mickiewicz[14] and was situated on the Ulica Grodzka[15]. For me this meant a daily walk across the rynek[16], at eight in the morning when the locals could be seen, hurrying to work and

10 Traditional potato-flour dumplings stuffed with cheese and onion

11 Beer

12 Our gang

13 Hello in Polish

14 A renowned writer

15 Grodzka Street

16 Main Square

re-stocking the much frequented bars, cafes and restaurants in the central square and a very different walk in the early evening when the strolling tourists would take-over. Kraków is the only city I have seen, apart from London, where there is no noticeable ebb and flow of tourism in the rynek – come snow or sun, they are out in their droves. This is potentially annoying if you live in the city, but it does mean that there are lots of young international people to feed the club and bar scene.

One particular club which stood out was the legendary 'Kitsch' which has since made it's way into the guidebooks and the news. The huge concrete staircase where we had stood many a time in gridlocked traffic collapsed in November of 2010, leaving eleven injured and 2,000 evacuated. When we first started going, there was only the occasional arrow sticker on a street corner as a clue to finding it. This towering building housed three different musical offerings from rock to cheese to pop heaven. It was a health and safety nightmare with no visible fire escape routes, a murky interior and three storeys of beer-coated, narrow stairways. A grimy fest of sweat, smoke and terrible music usually playing the same tunes repeatedly, so why did we go almost every night? Because it was at 'Kitsch' that I discovered it did not take chemical substances to dance until 6 a.m.!

Aside from the partying, Kraków inspired me to explore its crevices, which are full of tiny coffee shops where you can imagine ladies in velvet gloves smoking dainty cigarettes out of long holders. Detta and I decided to be cultured by agreeing on one night a week when we played chess in a coffee shop or bar – the loser had to buy the beers. One of the interesting things we found, was how many men would stare in disbelief at two young women using their brains. Sometimes they were polite and asked if they could watch, others just hovered around us, and some directly informed us of what our next play should be, presuming of course, that we were in desperate need of help. In the main however, we met some locals and made some friends this way (with a few checkmates being avoided). Although – truth be told, it was admittedly fun to shock people – it was only men who seemed to react, I do not recall a woman ever studying us like evolving monkeys in a zoo. The implications are quite worrying. Are women not expected to be able to play chess? Has our media promotion of bimbos lowered women's image? Or do two people sitting and playing a game seem old-fashioned now – would it be less conspicuous if we had our heads plugged into game consoles? I know that at my brother's school for example (he is eight), there is no chess club and he will not readily play a board game. Understandably he prefers to run around with his Nintendo Wii, than listen to his big sister laboriously explain how the horse is different from the rook.

Our group of friends all came together at different times in life, in order to take the next step in meeting ourselves. Poland gave us all a wonderful experience, a sense of connection to our roots that reached beyond childhood and family and into an immediate contemporary experience. The school part was more demanding than I had anticipated. I thought I was getting a break from serious study, but the Polish system is more rigorous than our own. I now thoroughly understand the widespread use of sciagi[17] by students of all ages in Poland. We were in the classroom from eight-thirty sharp for 'meldowanie', or the roll-call ritual with Pan Pyzik (the best wychowawca[18] if you are ever going to do the course, pray to be in his class), sometimes until seven at night.

'The Snobs' are all in touch, we have planned several big reunions over the years, the most important is for Ania's wedding in two years time. The week when everyone left was full of tears but also of laughs, at how lucky we were to have taken the decision to come back to the native land when we did. Certainly, Kraków marked a before and after for each of us. For me, it was a reminder that there are wonderful people all over the world, who can be found on many different paths. My conviction to step out and dare to try my dreams has led me to a cottage in a remote Scottish hamlet, from where I write this. Once you've heard the call of the wild it's enough to set you out on a journey. The wind

17 Cheat notes

18 Tutor

howls at the windows and the dogs sleep at my feet. I must still be young because my excitement is greater than my anxiety. I feel I have arrived. The voice in my head tells me: "I belong to be here." And so begins my Scottish life.

The Snob club

The Call of the Wild

What is home? Is it a place? Is it a feeling? Is it the people? I'm still looking for answers. I must have some Gypsy blood as my suitcase never gathers dust...I've heard that some people are homesick all their lives. Sitting on the train, going pretty much nowhere, with my diploma in my pocket, I was nervously biting my nails and looking around, I realised that life was not in good health. My life. The professional and the romantic. It was to be the end of the world according to Mayan prophecies, but it seemed like it was only the end of my preconceived ideals of success; the great job, the flat by the river and all the urban pleasures.

Remembering something from an American literature lecture, I went in search of Emerson's 'Nature' as a remedy; I felt in need of a soul-cleanse and a break from consumerism, (because even if we do not want to be, we are all products of our commercial environment). A nature where 'standing on the bare ground'; 'all mean egotism vanishes', and we become 'part and parcel of God', truly able to meet ourselves. A nature in which 'nothing can befall [one] in life...which nature cannot repair'.[19] I feel that we need to go back to basics as a culture in order to keep our cultural heritage in the shared psyche, so that we remember how to live from the land, repair old socks and very importantly, how to make vodka!

I cannot say for certain which happened first...the recognition of the desire to try a different life, or the way my partner and I kind of stumbled into each other's lives. I was fresh out of

19 http://www.chebucto.ns.ca/Philosophy/Sui-Generis/Emerson/quotes.htm>

university, and still religiously wore a hat whenever I didn't see the need to wash my hair. I hadn't more than my collection of English literature books to my name and was famed for carting about my worldly possessions in my silver suitcase which accompanied me on all adventures. At exactly this moment of precipices, cross-roads, indecision and endless possibilities, I encountered a towering, handsome and much older Scotsman. The attraction was immediate…chemistry led the way. So the 'one' finally arrived in my life! I was travelling on cloud nine and painting rainbows in the sky. The euphoria I was feeling defied all logic, the world was suddenly a much friendlier place, strangers were beautiful and spring appeared in the middle of winter! We each had what the other wanted. We were in love.

I like to think that our home found us. My partner's father told us about an old cottage he had watched for years with a view to moving into, but it never seemed the right time. It had been standing empty for a year in a tiny hamlet that time forgot. We went to view 'Ladyholm' on a bleak and chilly winter's day. The house seemed to reflect the milieu outside and did not inspire us. The ceilings felt low and constricting, the house felt dark and damp, as though it existed in permanent dusk – not to mention it's state of disrepair. Nature had begun to claim the garden back for herself and the key to open the door could serve as a hefty weapon. Old, musky furniture solemnly adorned the inside, outdated and unused. We both left with a similar impression.

However, over the next days I noticed that Ladyholm became a presence in my thoughts, my dreams. I wanted to reanimate the house; to paint it and fill it with laughter and fresh flowers, it seemed such a shame for it to stand empty, falling deeper into neglect. Initially I did not share my thoughts with William, but slowly it emerged that the house had captured his imagination also. We decided to commit ourselves to one-year of (each other) and the country-side (to start with). Suddenly, I am filled with a deep respect for all those people who slave away at their dream home for years like the unsung heroes in the programme 'Grand Designs'. Our project was only to make the house habitable, which took a couple of weeks. I was in my creative element, I was building a nest. Our daily mantra over coffee was: Make the place you live the place you love, whilst admiring our twig-spun heart hanging over the table.

Although my partner William is a Scotsman who has lived 'nearly' in the country his whole life and is far more practical than myself, he has never attempted total immersion before! Naturally, being a London girl (much as I hate to admit it), I find myself also without a clue as to when one should plant vegetables or how to sand floors. As I walk through the meadows, I think of Thomas Hardy's rural England and expect to see Tess of the d'Urbervilles coming round the corner. The state of the house means that the rent is within our budget and having put so much effort into making it a home, we actually arrived into the space long before the furniture did. I sit writing at William's grandfather's bureau by the window and although I am typing rather than scratching with a feather, history surrounds me. Our home sits on a river and is leased by an old lady who lives in Australia (the perfect landlady – no surprise home visits likely!) The name Ladyholm dates back to the Knights Templars of the 14th Century; a religious military order which protected pilgrims. The ladies, presumably nuns, who attended to the Knights would sleep at our house whilst on pilgrimages around the sacred wells in the area.

William's dog Caine, a nine-year-old-chocolate coloured Doberman was enjoying life in the wilderness as much as we were at first, he could at last stretch his legs in the back garden. Yet, as time went on, we felt that he may desire a companion. Each night we closed the kitchen door on a lonely looking Caine. He had been walked for his nine years round a busy loch each day where he could socialise with friends, but out here, there was only us and rabbits. And so began the quest for Caine's girlfriend. We found what we thought would be a suitable match in age and truth be told, colour, on the internet. The bitch was of the rare 'Isabella' colour, which is a sandy grey, so named after Isabella Archduchess of Austria who vowed not to change her underwear until her father Phillip II of Spain had taken Ostend in 1601. As the story goes, the Siege lasted some three years and Isabella emerged with sandy coloured petticoats and under-garments, not to mention a rancid perfume!

We packed Caine into the car and set off on the long drive south into England. Something of a collector's item in the dog world, 'Pepper' was definitely for the connoisseur, as she did not look like a Doberman, lacking the characteristic markings. The brief courtship seemed to go well – no teeth were shown as mutual sniffing took place. Caine seemed satisfied and William was pleased with this rarity.

The drive was long and the day hot, so we decided to let the dogs out of the car at a service stop along the motorway. Before we could grab her, the bitch shot out of the boot and along the motorway out of sight. Caine stood looking in bemusement between his fleeing future and us. What could we do? Poor Caine, she would rather run the gauntlet, criss-crossing a five lane motorway than be with him. I thought of the legendary Wanda, daughter of King Krakus who chose death over marrying a German, (Caine's illustrious pedigree traces back into European bloodlines), perhaps Pepper preferred to sacrifice herself rather than join with Caine? I remember being sat down by my Ciocia[20] when I was dating a German man, as she recounted the legend in a distinctly serious manner, reminding me that Wanda would not have thrown herself into the Wisła[21] for nothing and that we should learn from history. (It turned out that my romance was indeed short-lived, but thankfully with less dramatic consequences!) Disheartened with the loss of the dog, we continued into Scotland. Things did not look good for Caine.

We pondered on why she chose such a drastic measure – had he not been to her liking? We had not thought to wash him before the date, maybe that was the problem – but so much so that she felt the need to bolt up the motorway?! Perhaps she just did not see herself as a Scottish 'lass', knowing what a long history of

20 Aunty

21 Vistula River, the largest in Poland

bloodshed existed between the English and the Scots and fearing a frosty reception of blue-painted dogs screaming "Freedom!"?! Thankfully the dog was found by her previous owner a week later. (Needless to say he did not want to deliver her into our care again.)

Much of the joy seems to have left Caine's walks. He is inconsolable, as are we. The full impact of the incident has settled on the occupants of Ladyholm and the house no longer rings out with laughter and barking. Walks are carried out perfunctorily and dinners eaten for subsistence rather than pleasure. We need a 'lonely hearts' column for pets: mature male with gentle nature seeks companion who must share pastimes which include long woodland walks, hunting game and relaxing by the fire.

Caine remains a bachelor as yet and in the meantime we are distracting ourselves with jobs in the garden. We are aiming for as much self-sufficiency as we can manage with the resources we have. A section of the garden was designated for vegetables and rotavated with a prehistoric looking machine which ran William round the garden! When one is new at something, life sometimes throws in some luck as encouragement in the new undertaking. I decided to visit my father, who lives two hours away from us. William was in garden when I left. I later received a phone call to say that the entire vegetable patch was sown with potatoes, or 'tatties' as he calls them. The patch is approximately ten square metres – I am not an expert, but I was worried by this news – by my calculations this would be a serious amount of potatoes and I know of no way to preserve them... I estimated it would be about five potatoes to a plant, but I have since been told that it could be more like ten. In a patch that size, there could be anything up to twenty-four plants, yielding a crop of 240 – what were we going to do with all those potatoes?! It turns out that this was the best thing William could have done.

Potatoes clean the soil and should always be planted during the first year on new land. They are of course fine to eat as well. If you want to grow other things there is the option of grow bags which could not be simpler, just lay the bag on a flat surface, cut a hole in the plastic and plant seeds of your choice. Oh yes, and then the waiting with dirt-stained stained nails, (always the way to tell a true green-fingered compatriot as it is impossible to clean it all out!).

Caine waits for love, we wait for something, anything to rise out of the soil and the grow bags. Our life here resembles the 'Good Life' (the television programme), about a couple who are trying to be self-sufficient much to the amusement of their ridiculing friends. Many friends have been surprised by our sudden commitment to Ladyholm, wondering if we will feel isolated or bored – some even fear they have lost us to lunacy or hippy-dom. Not yet anyway.

A depressed Caine

Ladyholm

The Goat Chronicles

Ears

The goathouse

For several months now I have been inhabiting a new reality. I went from party-loving city girl – to rosy-cheeked country bumpkin in a couple of months. Sometimes I wake up in the morning and I cannot believe that this is my life, it feels simultaneously so grounded and yet, so surreal. It's not that I don't still enjoy a party or dressing up, but there is something far more fulfilling in the simple tasks of country life. By far the most disconcerting phenomena is the way time seems to pass more slowly, and yet in a day it does not seem possible to accomplish much more than walking the dog and cooking the day's repasts. All of a sudden, I become tired with the fading sun and able to rise with the dawn of a new day – this is all very new to me. In the past I have preferred a rather more nocturnal mode of existence (my room at university was referred to as 'the den'), but apparently all that can change. William, Caine, and I have all settled into the rhythms of life at Ladyholm.

I had always entertained the idea of living in the country. In my somewhat romanticised version of 'Old Macdonald's Farm', I was certain that I wanted to have goats. I had visions of walking through yellow, sun-ripened wheat fields leading beautiful goats through the long grass. I cannot be entirely sure what this random affinity was based on – I certainly admire the powers of endurance required to exist in their chosen habitats which consist of the most mountainous and rugged regions. I was able to observe them in their natural environment in Greece, where I was lucky enough to have slept under the stars whilst exploring the islands. On one island in particular, Ikaria, which has a lenient relationship with free-campers, we climbed up into the hills and slept in the open by cascading waterfalls, only emerging for tiropita (cheese pastry), batteries (for music) and ouzo (aniseed flavoured Greek spirit).

The island of Ikaria and the Ikarian Sea are named after the legendary Ikarus, whose father Daedalus fashioned wings of feather and wax in order to escape from King Minos. Deadalus and Ikarus were imprisoned because Deadalus had given Ariadne, the daughter of King Minos, some string, which saved Theseus from the Minotaur in the labyrinth. Daedalus warned his son not to fly too close to the sea or the sun, but, intoxicated by the freedom of flying and the beautiful views over the island (I would imagine), Ikarus became distracted and melted his wings. According to legend, Ikarus fell to his death in the sea. We slept in hammocks and were only woken by the bells of mountain goats on their way up through the ravines – that was when I understood that there are places on this earth where only goats can go. They won my respect and curiosity – I am also a Capricorn, but that may have less to do with it. As much as I may like to imagine myself as a graceful and athletic gazelle-goat mix, I am not sure that this would be my totem in the animal world. Embarrassingly, I am known as the 'sloth' between friends!

I recently discovered a quality which my partner and his son both share, in a valuable lesson. In the most reductionist view of human nature, we can divide people between those who are 'doers' and those who are 'talkers' (they only pontificate aloud, often in abundance but with little physical effect). I happened to mention over dinner that I adored goats, in a relevant conversation about animals. Two days later we received a phone-call. William's son had found two lady goats, called 'nannies', as a present. It was then I realised that I had better be careful what I say around the two of them, because they possess the uncommon ability to simply *manifest*. The saying 'Be careful what you wish for' has never been truer, because you just might get it and you may have no idea what it really means!

The goats have a rather interesting story. If we had not agreed to take them in, they were going to be killed. There was about a week in between us hearing of the goats and them physically appearing. They arrived out of a trailer, one white and brown with beautiful markings and perfectly formed horns, the other was black with a little white, but she was not able to stand and walk out of the trailer. She looked strange, her head had two big lumps where her ears should have been and huge wounds all over her little body. We could not believe that anyone would transport or give away animals in that state. For farmers she was just an animal. I cried. She had been savaged by a dog a few days prior to her arrival. The dog must have been the size of a wolf: she was in the worst state I have seen a creature in. She could not stand, her head was bloody and sore, her eyes were clouded over, there was a piece of hard, black flesh, which I diagnosed as gangrene, still hanging on to her head and her coat was falling out. We were convinced that she was going to die, that the universe had sent her to us, to make her a soft straw bed, give her water and let her pass on.

Initially, on account of our inexperience, the goats colonised their own Garden of Eden. They roamed free in our large garden which runs all the way around the house and had our company which they demanded much of the time. These early days, like every novelty, were magical. We watched them with wonderment eating, climbing trees and drinking with their funny little tongues, often spying on them from the kitchen window. Caine was banished to a tiny portion of the garden for his unclear motives. He was constantly trying to get close to the goats in displays of running and barking, which made them nervous and Caine slightly unpredictable, on the one hand his wagging three-vertebrae-long tail indicated friendliness, yet on the other, his snapping teeth spelled dinner.

We were especially hard on Caine because we could see the amount of stress his presence caused both goats. Sometimes however, when he did get close, he thankfully he left the wounded one alone. I wonder if nature told him that she was not a fair fight. It is definite, that a goat with horns against a large dog is a fair match, either could win with different merits. Whenever Caine got too frisky, he received a few short, sharp blows from the horns. This was particularly effective when she cornered him against a wall or fence (which he could easily have jumped!) For a while this was a game which the goat enjoyed a little too much and she would chase Caine around the garden. There were no naming ceremonies as yet because we thought we would lose the little goat.

The goats were able to seek shelter in an old wood shed with a roof, but we had no idea what we ought to feed them, if we could milk them or if they needed a proper house. Goats, like all grazing animals, are able to completely decimate an area before moving, because nature drives them relentlessly on to younger shoots and leaves. The more I think about it, we as a species completely destroy our surroundings by cutting down trees, dirtying water and pumping pesticides all over the land, full-well knowing that we will stay where we are. Goats are driven by instinct, they always move on – their droppings fertilise future plants and the foliage grows again – what is our excuse?

Soon, there were tiny pellets, like those rabbits produce, all over the garden. We began to feel like the goats ruled the outside space. In a final display of power the goat with horns jumped onto the outside table and looked straight into the window when she knew we were watching, as though to say – "I claim this table."

In the mean-time, I have been studying nutritional healing, which looks at using food, spirituality and emotional stability to create a well-balanced picture of health. One of the best things you can do for your body is actually to jump on a 'rebounder' (sounds expensive, but it is just a trampoline), for thirty minutes a day if you can manage it. The reason being that the jumping moves the lymph and stimulates the circulation in a more dynamic way than for example step-aerobics does. It is not as easy as you may think – we bought a ten foot trampoline which lives in the garden and we have been trying to jump on it every day to earn our meals. You can take my word for it – it's exhausting! The goats also seemed to like the idea of jumping and nibbling what tiny green shoots we were lovingly watering in our vegetable garden, half of which is planted in grow bags. Goats will eat anything, whether it be flowers, weeds or clothes! As I sat surrounded by empty bags of earth where our future broccolis should have been, I sought refuge in a glass of wine and a cigarette as I waited in trepidation to tell William the news. As I sat, looking at the bottle, I noticed that it had a picture of a goat on it – as if they had not done enough damage already! The man at the wine shop in our nearest town recommended it to me, as I usually choose wine on whether I like the label, but this has become increasingly difficult with new world wines, as the labels are often uninteresting and very shiny. This was the end of that era for the goats and the end of my wine ignorance!

The wounded goat was eating, drinking and producing a strange sound which we thought maybe due to the fact that she cannot hear and her 'maaa' is distorted making her sound like something out of 'Star Wars'. She came back to life, slowly, tentatively standing, walking a little, becoming a goat again. At nutritional school, they teach us that when we are sick the best thing we can do is observe a dog – when he is sick, he only drinks water, fasts and sleeps. Whenever I am sick, my Mamusia[22] in true Polish character feeds me rosoł[23], black tea and kaszki[24]. If you need to eat when you are unwell, then all kaszki are fantastic; millet, buckwheat, pearl barley. Apparently though, food does not give us energy – in a healthy person 70% of energy should be made from *light* alone. Food nourishes us with vitamins and minerals, but when was the last time you ate a meal and felt like going to the gym? Digestion diverts blood and water from other duties and our organism can only do one of two things at one time – restore and repair or defend against bacteria/illness. With the goat eating, she was going to survive and she needed a name. A friend of ours came round for dinner and being a film maker, he suggested that we call the wounded goat 'Ears', like in an Italian mafia film, where the character called 'Fingers' has none. We liked the idea, so we now have 'Horns' and an ironically named 'Ears' – the gangster!

Whilst walking Caine I often think back to 'running the gauntlet' of Hyde Park's big dogs which my terrier much loved to attack – to the anger and dismay of other dog owners. I think we never really get to know a breed of dog until we have grown to love one of its kind. In my mind, Dobermans always had a 'tough-guy' image. When my parents and I decided on our first dog, it was because I had always wanted one and happened to talk to a friend of the family who bred border terriers. I was convinced from that moment on that this was what we needed to get, they are small dogs, which we thought would be more manageable in a London

---

22 Diminutive of Mum in Polish, Mummy

23 Polish chicken soup

24 Wholegrains

Horns

flat. It seems that the bigger the dog the less aggressive, the better it is disciplined and the less unpredictability. I would have gladly traded in some of my terrier's quirks for a quieter life! A terrier is what you call a value for money dog – it has enough stamina, guts and machismo for several big dogs. Yes, there's no doubt that in every terrier's mind lives the self-image of a lion, whereas, in the

Doberman, it seems there lives a much more gentle creature who is just as loving but not a victim of 'little man' syndrome!

Visits from Mamusia and the Polish contingent brighten our times here. From the second she arrives there is a flurry of activity, from cooking to complete reorganisation of the kitchen. Mamusia spends much of her time with her glasses on, digging in the attic amongst all the books and furniture which belong to the landlady. She periodically comes running down the stairs with dusty books in her hands, asking which one I think is valuable. She is on a hunt for the biały kruk [25]which she is certain she can sense amongst the cobwebs. A Polish Mamusia is a wonderful asset, she has an answer for everything and an innate knowing of how things should be (whether one should wear their hair up or down, how many times a day to feed animals, how to lose weight, the meaning of life – the list is endless). I often wonder if all this information is downloaded from the collective wisdom of our species when a woman becomes a Mamusia (I am counting on this, which is probably why I would like to have five children!)

On account of there being no replies to Caine's lonely-heart advert, the nine-year bachelor, (well perhaps not completely, but nothing long-lasting), is still in search of a companion, perhaps even a bride as he is getting too old to play hard to get. After the last disastrous attempt at match-making, we decided not to be too hasty. It seems that dog-courtship like our own, needs time to blossom into something different – whether this ends with; a smile (display of sharp teeth), complete indifference, or some frolicking in the grass rests on the delicate matter of body-language. The search continues …

---

25 A very valuable old book

Caine Meets His Match and Zosia Ponders on Scottish Soil

The Falls of the River Clyde at New Lanark

Instead of waking up to the smell of percolating coffee and hot chocolate for my darling Scotsman, I find myself nervously reaching for a cigarette and listening for sounds of life from the other room. Despite our knowledge on dealing with issues; namely airing problems on the line, we have been taking them as they arise, to separate bedrooms for a night of sulking... Nothing. William must have already gone to work. It is a lonely morning walk with the dogs for me, full of speculation on what he is thinking, when he will come home and how we will melt the ice. I throw myself into 'housewife' tasks to escape my thoughts. After a long wait and much fretting, William walks into the kitchen. We both try to remain composed because the moment feels like it requires severity, so we turn our faces away to smile (because really, we are pleased to see each other). Slowly we begin to talk, awkwardly at first, testing the waters – is it safe to be vulnerable? It is a unanimous decision and we clear the air.

As Ladyholm becomes a repository for our memories, slowly collecting our laughter, tears and moments, I think about how many other peoples' fates these walls hold. Our neighbour, a charming old man who lives just over the bridge quenched our curiosity with some local knowledge. A mother and daughter lived at Ladyholm until a disagreement led them not to speak to each other for years and the daughter emigrated to Australia. She refuses to sell the house, insisting on renting it until she passes, when she wishes it to be donated to charity. It is interesting how attached to sentiment we are – she is loath to let go of the memory of the house – yet she is too elderly to ever return to it. I often wonder if mother and daughter gave any thought to the future receivers of the fruit when they planted the apple tree in the garden – soon to be the only living thing which bears the fruit of their lives.

Now we have become familiar with the place, I have begun to observe the neighbours and I am wondering if the people make the place, or vice-versa? We have situated ourselves in our vision of paradise; rolling green hills, ancient twisted trees and wide open spaces which dwarf our existence. Yet, rather than the cheery, ruddy-cheeked country-folk I imagined to inhabit these pastures, I find our hamlet to be composed of eccentric and mysterious individuals. The farmer for example, who drives his tractors at seventy miles per hour around tiny country lanes, wearing an expression which suggests he only eats raw lemons and he would rather-run-you-down-than-stop-for-you-if the law did not expressly forbid it. I also spotted the Lady of the near-by manor at the petrol station. She sat, clasping her hands over her purse, in her lap in a vintage BMW, waiting for the man I know to be her ex-husband (thanks to the neighbour); they continue living together although they are now divorced. She is a beautiful and dignified blonde woman; in white driving gloves and a silent inaccessibility she wears around her like a crown. Her ex-husband seems a gentle man whom we once chanced upon, happily cutting the bushes to make park-like paths between fields where we walk our dogs. I had often wondered who maintained these secret gardens only for the pleasure of the rabbits and foxes.

When I first moved to Scotland at eighteen, having finished college, I imagined that I would find a land full of beautiful and courageous Mel Gibsons, as in *Braveheart*. Unfortunately, this was not the case. My father lives near an uneventful and grey town (I was of course comparing it to London), which is considered rather large because 'it has shops on both sides of the road'! This was a complete culture shock and I came face-to-face with the reality of people who far from living the country dream, live in city-sized houses or flats, surrounded by wilderness. They have none of the quirks of city life; one disco, a few pubs, a handful of shops and none of the advantages of country life with small or non-existent gardens. In this corner of the world the government pays for people to complete their driving licence, because without one, it is impossible to live.

Leaving London was traumatic; my Mama, Wujek[26], best friend and Russian sweetheart, all lined up on the pavement outside my shared flat. My father, having driven all the way from Scotland

26 Uncle

in his Range Rover was thoroughly excited by the prospect of taking his daughter home to live with him for the first time since my parents separated many years earlier. Unfortunately, looking back with the 20:20 vision of hindsight, this cannot have been the joyful homecoming he was envisioning. I was distraught; rivulets of mascara were coursing down my face at the thought of leaving behind my beloved family and friends. My trusty border terrier Bertie accompanied me on this adventure. As I waved goodbye to the people who had been the main characters in my life, I could not have known that I was waving goodbye to the protagonist who was to transform in the Scottish borders.

It turns out that I was not too far fetched with those fantasies of *Braveheart*, it just took a few years to find. On a routine trip to the Tesco in our nearest big town, I discovered that I was rubbing shoulders with history – on the main street in the town of Lanark, there stands a statue of William Wallace himself. The plaque on the same church testifies to holding the marriage ceremony of Wallace and his beloved Marion Braidfute. Wallace was an outlaw and it seems after further research, a bit of a rogue-cum-national hero, so how did the younger son of a Scottish Knight gain a title of notoriety through history? Scotland was conquered in 1296 by the English. Unsurprisingly, resentments did not take long to surface as many Scottish nobles were imprisoned, taxed and expected to serve King Edward I. In the revolts that broke out all over Scotland, William Wallace became a leader by slaying William Heselrig, the English Sheriff of Lanark. Many other military successes against the English followed and Wallace was knighted and named 'Guardian of Scotland' for his achievements. Naturally, the English history books chronicle Wallace as a brutal and barbarous outlaw, because history is written by the victorious.[27]

For variety in socialising, we walk Caine along the very banks of the Clyde where Wallace took shelter from the British. On one of these walks, secretly hoping that Caine would find a girlfriend,

27 <http://www.bbc.co.uk/history/scottishhistory/independence/features_independence_w...>

I strayed into New Lanark and discovered the legacy of Robert Owen. Owen was a social pioneer who believed in the equal education of all men, discounting race, colour or creed. He not only envisioned an egalitarian model of society, but he went a long way towards creating it by establishing New Lanark as a model community. Owen created a version of the Industrial Revolution which was mutually advantageous. New Lanark was the first to have an Infant School, a crèche for working mothers, free medical care and comprehensive education. The inhabitants of the town also benefited from concerts, dancing and nature.[28] It is well worth a visit, attracting many tourists each year and offering an award winning visitor centre.

The little houses are identical and plaques with Owen's creed are to be found around each corner, one reads: "It is therefore in the interest of all that everyone, from birth, should be well educated, physically and mentally, that society may be improved in its character." Unfortunately, many of the Scots are guilty of perpetuating the hatred of the English. I was recently at a Highland dance organised for tourists, in which my cousin, a professional student of ballet was participating. The show was traditional, filled with the haunting and resounding chime of bag pipes and punctuated by anti-English jokes. Although these never fail to draw a laugh from the tourists, I am wondering if there is any point in propagating a history so bloody and so far behind us. Thankfully I have not come across many negative responses once I open my mouth, which cannot hide its London roots. Scottish people on the whole are very friendly and charming with their reputably sexy accents. The Scots were once a famed fearless and tribal society whose power lay in their courage and strong family bonds. Why is it that heroes such as *Braveheart* are all anyone remembers and not the prophetic Robert Owens?

Our darling dog Caine has found love at last. Apparently all those years of bachelor status did nothing to reduce his charm and good looks, his lady is named Blue and she is a twenty-month

28 <http://www.robert-owen.com/>

old black and tan bitch. Caine, the old devil surprised us by finding such a young mate compatible. Blue came to us as a rescue from the Doberman Welfare Association, she could no longer be kept in her home because her sister, a brown Doberman like Caine, was neurotic, which resulted in fighting and vet's bills for her former owner. Blue's desire for closeness is illustrated by her constant attempts to climb into Caine's bed with him. Unfortunately we have not made this particularly easy for them because Blue's bed is in the pantry and Caine's is not big enough for the two of them. Watching them in their developing relationship has been a privilege, as their issues reflect our own. William and I were very speedy in taking the step of moving in together in our 'experiment'. The advantage of this is that we are still learning so much about each other. The disadvantage of this is that we are still learning so much about each other!

Proximity and the joys of cohabiting, eating off one another's plates and taking up the whole bed delight and dismay both Caine and his master. Clearly Blue assumes that Caine desires the same amount of closeness as she does, which leads her to follow him from his bed to hers where he craves to be left alone. This is where his lifetime (nine years) of solitude begins to show. On the human dimension, it seems that there are similar disparities – everyone is from a different home and has various ideas about how things should be. Whilst I know I am a messy person, I despise dirt. I used to joke with Mama about our perfect house – it would be almost bare of furniture, certainly have no wardrobes but a lot of floor space and the occasional chair for thrown clothes to opportunely land on!

I am discovering that William may not share the same fantasy, as he has begun to express some displeasure at my idea of 'tidy'. Thankfully, we both have similar hygiene standards and William is extremely domesticated, loving cooking and not being shy of cleaning. I definitely belong to the 'hamster' category of people who are unable to throw away accumulated 'stuff'; everything from useless gifts, sentimental nick-knacks and old receipts. William on the other hand has spent many years living the minimalist dream in bachelor pads. There is clearly some adjusting to do. If we want to live together, how are we going to do it? The much over-used solution for happiness – compromise springs to mind, but how exactly does it happen? It is not enough to make a commitment to be more understanding. How do we reach a solution that is workable for us both? I am thrown into pontificating on the nature of relationships. When we love, does the detail of a person enrich that love, or is it merely an accompaniment?

There have been a few lover's tiffs on the way, but now it seems that a solid love has grown between Caine and Blue. We have been camping, shown Blue the sea for the first time and watched them hunting. It seems that Blue – far smaller and faster on her feet than Caine, is a formidable hunter, almost every walk culminates in a poor, timorous beastie breathing it's last breath between Blue's razor sharp teeth. She seeks out, she pursues and she makes the kill, hunting anything in her path from; baby birds fallen from the nest, complacent rabbits, sluggish grouse and hedgehogs, who (rightly) think they are safe. Due to her exceptionally soft mouth, she will and does carry the curled up and spiky creatures all the way home, where at last, she has to admit defeat – there is no way to penetrate that ball of spikes!

It seems that in a domestic setting, Blue is the boss, commanding any bed she pleases and even eating out of Caine's bowl, which we deemed unfair and separate rooms for eating have become a must if poor Caine is not to end up on a diet. Although, Blue may be trying to prove a point – Caine is rather chunky! However, once we leave the house the roles reverse and Caine becomes the unquestionable 'Boss' – once contented to pick up and crunch long-dead rabbits(much to our disgust), he now watches Blue make the kill and runs over for the lion's share. Blue immediately gives up her bounty and moves away. She will not return or bother her man until he is quite finished, at which point she is allowed over to investigate for any left-overs. The arrangement works rather well in Caine's favour, though the price is sharing his territory, especially his bed – "Hmmm, this gender role reversal with woman-as-bread-winner movement is rather good" – Caine thinks to himself! Walks are once again the pleasure of the day and Caine rewards us with an extra spring in his step and appreciative looks as he parades majestically in front of Blue.

In a bid of war against my lack of knowledge on wine, thanks to Mamusia, I have acquired some useful materials, which I have taken to consulting with a glass of wine in hand on an evening. I now know that Pinot Noir is the new craze, though not the cheapest option out there, you should expect to pay around £7-£8 for a good bottle and you need not go for the French variety as Chile and Southern Australia are also producing enticing offerings.

As much as I adore my country existence, there are occasional moments when I wonder what on earth I am doing in the middle of nowhere and how I ever thought I could survive here – far away from everything! It is in these moments, harried by the fluttering of my young heart, that I seek refuge on a bench at the foot of the garden where I can hear the river flowing, often in the company of a cigarette and a (well chosen) glass of wine. William's sanctuaries are trips on the motorbike, where he goes I can only wonder, but he returns sometimes after an hour, sometimes after a day's trip, refreshed and full of energy.

Blue and Caine

Caine and Blue in his bed

As I sit looking out into the viridescence of Scotland, I notice that not one but three families of birds have colonised our roof. I am thrilled because I believe this to be an auspicious sign of good fortune and their twitters are to be heard each morning. The smatterings of their droppings are not as lovely, but I am willing to deal with this side-effect. The advent of new life raises my spirits and reminds what time of year it is, because the weather would have me believe otherwise. The summer has been disappointing, the mornings usually bode well and invite dresses, but the afternoons bring downpours which swell our river. When we are lucky, the whole family (William, myself, Blue and Caine) all sit outside and enjoy our garden before the midges arrive and annoy us out of our serenity and sanity. Despite our eco-dreams, we have not quite managed self-sufficiency. Our own (plentiful) potatoes and courgettes alone cannot sustain us and we are forced to join the consumerist ways of our denaturalised society in a weekly stock-up at the shops.

However, some anonymous bundles have been arriving with our post, which have sustained us in our 'mission'. Every couple of weeks, tiny bundles appear, tied to the fence with our letters. The house is still very much a work in progress and a letter box has not made it to the top of the priority list yet, so we can see the squares of coarse linen, tied together with brown string from the bedroom upstairs. Each one contains tiny seeds, perfectly formed, of all shapes and colours, which put jelly beans to shame. At first, we thought it was a prank by our friends, but everyone swears to ignorance on the matter and it has been going on too long to be a joke. We are left wondering, by whose hand and with what intention these 'gifts' are appearing. Despite the mystery, we take encouragement from them and they warm some silent recesses of our hearts as we feel deeply encouraged in our daring to try a different lifestyle.

We are working on the fundamental issues which face men and women in relationships. As a teenager I always believed that age aided us in knowing when it is the right time to work things through and when it is the right time to say 'goodbye'. Unfortunately, as

I look around, it seems many people gain from age an ability to close their hearts sooner and say 'goodbye' quicker, without any of the blind idealism and hope of youth which is necessary to maintain the magic of love. I am learning that talking lengthily about issues is the greatest testament to commitment. Every crossroads we come to provides us with the opportunity to walk another step deeper into facing the other and ultimately ourselves, because the other is a beautiful mirror for us, reflecting all our shortcomings and our qualities. The spare room has been banished as a method of avoiding issues, with a heavy padlock which can be opened by two keys. Hopefully we have learned a lesson and we soldier on...

The Island of Lesbos

A Long Way From Home

The decision to leave behind my country home and participate in a therapist training course during the summer was born out of the desire to improve myself as a person. It is my belief, that without self-awareness we are not able to function in the world as it really is, without becoming completely lost in our own dramas which we orchestrate. I am no stranger to working with the body and mind, having been introduced to body-psychotherapy as a rebellious teenager. At that time it seemed completely unnecessary and totally insane, however, I believe that it has made me who I am today, and most importantly: still alive. The reality of growing up a 'mongrel' with a Polish mother and an English father in cosmopolitan London promoted a wonderful equality in multiculturalism. We 'mieszanki' or mongrels are a breed of our own, enriched with a double cultural heritage, we are blessed and yet we are often lost in confusion. The need for an absolute identity particularly during teenage years can plunge us into a rejection of one or other culture, language and parent, causing a deep schism in the psyche. By not accepting them, we are not accepting ourselves.

Often, we believe we are acting from our conscious mind which has the best intentions, however: our unconscious motivations can sabotage our best efforts. How many times have you been baffled at a pear-shaped situation, or someone else's reaction to you? With a bit of help, we can begin to clear away some of the cobwebs and familiarise ourselves with our inner terrain. Hopefully, we become aware of what we are *actually* sending out into the world, rather than what we think we are, because the two may be at loggerheads. One of the things which I have discovered on the journey of self-awareness, is that I favour working with the body, or the body-mind (which relies on the natural intelligence stored within your cells), rather than cognitive therapy. The main reason for this preference is that I find the mind to be such a tricky character, however, it does not have the ability to control what the body may unearth in a session because the body does not lie. It can only experience what is already there.

I cannot omit that I agreed to diving into this adventure after being persuaded by my father's enthusiasm to experience something new together. It was supposed to be a bonding and learning opportunity. However, at the last moment something came up at work, so it was just me and my silver suitcase. After changing planes in Athens I arrived on the mythical island of Lesbos. Following a two-hour hair-raising taxi drive along mountain precipices with sheer cliff faces and foaming waves many feet below, I was left wondering how explorers ever felt inspired to explore the Greek islands. Lesbos like many of the other islands I have visited looks from the outside like a giant rock, craggy and barren scorched by the sun and pounded by the relentless waves. Yet, once penetrated, these islands house beautiful oases of lush vegetation and sandy beaches. Being a rather large island, Lesbos has an airport and a road which runs it's perimeter. Following in the footsteps of the famous poetess Sappho, who brought lesbianism its name, the island has become a gay mecca frequented each year by countless tourists.

Just in case I had any dreams of a paradisiacal month spent by the sea, they were quickly dispelled upon arrival at the centre where the course was held. This training was a month of Reichian body work. This particular one was in a form called 'Pulsation', led by a woman with a lifetime of experience in the field. Wilhelm Reich was a student of Freud's, who found that classic psychoanalysis was not always achieving results. Typically, the patient lays on the couch and talks without ever seeing the therapist who sits behind them, in order to minimise the effects of transference and counter-transference. Reich began to notice similarities amongst clients; they all reported dysfunctional or non-existent sexual lives, breathed in a shallow way and seemed disconnected from their bodies. He started to experiment by asking them to breathe deeply and systematically into the belly, diaphragm and chest. His patients began to tap into and release various tensions and traumas, leaving them freer and less inhibited. This led Reich to map the muscular armouring of the body, in which different segments of muscles work together in holding and suppressing emotions and tensions. With so much energy devoted to 'holding things together', very little energy is left for the enjoyment of living, spontaneity and the 'juiciness' of our sensual experience. The senses are a fundamental condition of our lives on earth, which we often negate due to our societal conditioning, resulting in painful and diseased bodies because of stagnated energy.

This month was one of the most testing experiences I have encountered. The training consisted of sessions beginning at 7 am with an active meditation called 'dynamic', followed by a break for breakfast and a quick shower. The morning session consisted of a warm-up and more intense body work, leading to lunch. The afternoon session was more of the same, ending with two meditations before dinner at 9 pm – the 'kundalini' and the 'white robe'[29] active meditations. The night session after dinner was usually a lighter one, consisting either of a sharing about the days explorations, or theory, bringing the day to a close at around midnight. I was expecting an intense process, it is body work after all, but this was extreme, even as the youngest person in the group it was a stretch. I was in awe of the oldest man in our group who was eighty years old, with one eye, who attended all sessions and meditations, dancing and laughing all the while. Wow! What an inspiration, life energy was clearly flowing through him, I can only hope we will all have such a zest for life at that age. The routine was rigorous; leaving me with blistered feet, a lip full of cold sores (literally), and calf muscles so tight I was hobbling around like an old woman after the first week! Vanity was impossible, I have never

29 Both types of meditations were developed by the mystic Osho, designed to help Westerners especially escape from the busyness of the mind

gone for so long without looking in a mirror, applying makeup, or generally caring what I looked like! It was actually incredibly liberating I have to say, not to think about any everyday rituals.

The teaching was world class, we received lessons and booklets on anatomy and Reich's theories, which extended far and wide. He diagnosed a system of body types (which Alexander Lowen later developed), based on physical appearance, emotional tendencies and intellectual strategies. However, the main focus was on experiential learning, we were exchanging sessions with each other daily, in the role of therapist/client in a giant laboratory, free to experiment and guided by skilful assistants. The idea was to work with a different person each day, in order to see how different we all are, and yet there are certain systems within the body which function universally, for example; two basic ones are tension and stress stored in the shoulders and anger in the jaw, hence the expression 'through gritted teeth'.

It was possible to survive the training itself, however, the setting was a process all of its own. Although I was somewhat angry at my dad for not coming, I could not possibly have imagined him there. The commune was made up of supposedly like-minded people and a condition of stay was working through a morning break every other day. We were assigned the kitchen (which consisted in washing plates and cutlery in cold water from a hose), course room or bar area each day. A taxi-ride away from the beach, down dusty dirt roads, where not even goats roamed due to a lack of vegetation; it felt like a desert complete with scorpions (with a non-lethal sting, but scorpions nonetheless). The place is pervaded by a 'wildness' and run by Greek men. It is a brand of spirituality and a lack of hygiene which is not to all tastes.

There seemed to be many men just hanging around, observing the people, coming and going, which contributed to a sexual atmosphere. The bar was a hit-and-miss affair – it was sometimes open during breaks, sometimes serving fruit and sometimes inexplicably abandoned. In a break it was possible to have a coffee, a cigarette, an alcoholic drink and a sexual encounter. This was the part I was uncomfortable with, it seemed that some people congregated at the commune, to flirt and socialise, leading to an environment of promiscuity and something of a hippy style 'free love' vibe. Any processes I had participated in until then had been solely about the experience of the process itself, with rules of silence and sexual integrity. Any feelings or attractions which develop are picked up on and used as a vehicle for the individual to go deeper within themselves, observing how quickly we want to project on the outer world so as to avoid a deep meeting with self. Here, anything goes. Talking, provocative clothes and full contact – I observed the combination with emotional work was quite explosive!

People within this world had taken ancient Sanskrit names to signify their rebirth into a life characterised by a pursuit of personal liberation. Defenders of this style of life say that it brings process into real life with a focus on personal responsibility, rather than it being something completely cut off from a reality which must be returned to. I understand this line of thought and I believe this world to be a wonderful place of physical liberation for highly repressed people, or those who for example, did not experiment in their teens. It is just a question of taste.

I spoke to many people who had deeply transformational experiences in these communes and likewise, many who found it overwhelming and in some cases invasive. I certainly had to overcome my own shock, sense of threat and cynicism which always uttered an internal giggle when being introduced to European people whose names were clearly Anna, Peter or Kostas, presenting themselves with names such as 'Kali', 'Krishna' and 'Shiva'[30]. The idea that a new name makes a person more spiritual I find absurd. Would it make you more likely to help an old lady across the road with her shopping? In my experience this kind of renaming often simply inflates the spiritual ego. I also feel that accepting one's own birth name can be another important stepping stone on the way to self-acceptance.

One evening, I hovered at the bar, badly sunburnt, wearing a

30 Kali: Hindu goddess of destruction/death and rebirth. Krishna: Hindu god of compassion and love. Shiva: Hindu god of transformation

cardigan and shivering despite the thermal evening. I could feel the hot flushes and the chills beginning to wreak havoc on my skin. Where is she? I wondered to myself, I would just like to say 'Hello' and excuse myself. An older man, with a mane of unkempt curly hair turned to me – "Why are you wearing this?" he asked in a thick Greek accent, indicating my jumper. "Oh, I'm sunburnt." "Really?" His eyebrows went up, widening his eyes, seemingly connected to the corners of his mouth which had by now widened into a Cheshire Cat grin. "I have some special healing calendula oil in the kitchen, I could rub some into your back, my hands have healing properties," he said stubbing out his cigarette and waving them in front of my eyes. I could not have imagined anything worse than being carted off to the kitchen, completely abandoned at this time of night, to have 'healing' oil rubbed into my sore back by a sleazy old man. "Thank you, but I'm really alright, just waiting for my friend, she's playing music here in the bar tonight." He laughed to himself and stared straight ahead, as though seeing through me in some way.

I had the constant feeling that my restraint was perceived as frigidity by the people at the commune, that I was comical, like the new kid at school who has not yet learned what is cool. Completely undeterred, I remained standing and shivering while my companion, a moment ago so full of generosity, treated me as a fly on the wall. I have never been much good at going to a bar or restaurant and dining or drinking alone. I always associate it with the loneliness of civilised life, all the people who buy meals for one in the supermarket, living their solo lives – a far cry from the tribal communities we came from. Lacking other company, I asked my companion, "What's your name?" I should have guessed what was coming, his round, pink face turned once again to me as he heavily proclaimed that his Sanskrit name meant 'the god of love' and that no other seeker bears that name. Inwardly smirking I wondered if he like so many others had christened himself. I asked. "Of course not, how vain would I have to be to give myself this name, I was given it." Ok, I thought, probably by your best friend! The 'god of love' had now worryingly turned to face me and I could feel the full weight of his attention, studying me. I looked into the shadows of the outdoor bar, wishing someone I knew would show up. Feeling that the 'god of love' was still imagining I might be persuaded into his massage, I asked, "What do you do?" He turned away from me and lit another cigarette, inhaling deeply and slowly, he exhaled just as languorously. "I give light." He said, delivered in true New Age ethereal style. I could not help the chortle which escaped me – "What do you actually do?" I asked sarcastically by this point, wondering how people can stand communicating in such an ungrounded way about the most ordinary things. "I'm an electrician," he said turning to face the bar. I laughed and this signalled the end of the exchange.

The place was peopled by a colourful array of nationalities which I found fascinating. In a group of twenty-odd I found several Slavs, Russians, a Bosnian woman, a Czech man and a compatriot – I was delighted to find Mariola, a Polish woman living in India. The extent of the Polish diaspora never ceases to amaze me! Although they all move in the circles of this commune world, I found several wonderful friends with whom I am still in contact. Occasionally, we decided that a trip to the beach in the afternoon and a little evening dance in the town were just as beneficial as a meditation in the commune.

For me the experience was a real test of endurance and character. I returned home feeling detoxed in my body, the sweating and body work had burnt out a lot of toxins, my skin was feeling new and clean and I felt motivated to keep up the cleansing. On an emotional level, I felt like I had more space inside, more distance from the chatter of the mind and a confidence coming from feeling a connection with my inner self. Although I returned feeling strong, exhausted and exhilarated, grateful for my experiences and the people I connected with, I do not imagine that I will be visiting this commune again. I have never missed Bonny Scotland, my Scotsman and my dogs so much! The warrior is awakened, able to survive anything now.

Ears the goat

The End of a Goat Era

Soon after returning home from the interesting journey in Greece, I realised that my darling had been sparing me some of the realities of his daily life for the month of my absence. Bright and chirpy the morning after my arrival home, William is readying himself for work. As I sleepily mumble: "I'll walk the dogs today." I am surprised that I receive a pat on the head and strict instructions to rest. As William walks out of the bedroom he casually says, "Just put the goats out when you surface." I happily return to napping, feeling like a lady of leisure. It seemed that no sooner had I dropped off to sleep, than I began to hear a sound which rudely intruded on my dreams, like a demented Chewbacca…

Running downstairs in my attractive rozowy frotkowy szlawroczek[31], hard as sand-paper after so many years of use, I tear outside to see what unearthly creature has colonised my garden. I find one goat manically smashing her head into the fence of her sleeping barn and as I look around to locate her companion I nearly have a heart attack! There is a fully grown Galloway blackhead cow standing my garden and a goat in my vegetable patch surrounded by half-consumed gardening utensils. Now, knowing as I do that a couple of people are killed each year by cows in Scotland whilst trying to save their dogs, I wisely grab my two by the scruff of the neck (figuring that the goats can fend for themselves). Whilst in the precarious position of protecting my modesty and screaming unavailingly, a neighbour casually strolls past, getting an eyeful of the spectacle.

---

31 Pink towelled dressing gown

The island of Lesbos seems an age away as I run into the kitchen with a face as red as a burak[32] and light up a cigarette: the dogs are barking, one goat is trying to escape, the other is snacking on my organic vegetables and 'Daisy' the gargantuan cow is standing ominously in the garden – what on Earth can I do? Many unhelpful thoughts flash through my mind, mainly with the flavour of 'How did a girl from London get herself into this?!' Or 'I wish I had a few tranquiliser darts!'

Ungrateful savages – we nursed the goats back to health, loved and cared for them, how did they become such megalomaniacs? The goats who by this point, require daily tethering thanks to their ability to; jump, eat or trample any enclosure attempts, have become an absolute nightmare. Terrified to go outside, I quickly throw on some clothes and decide there is nothing for it – I have to get myself to the pub in town if I have any hope of tracking down the farmer, who may otherwise wait days to check that herd. I escape through the front door into my post-box red-eco-mobile and drive at lighting speed to the nearest town.

Thankfully, the two Polish girls I have befriended are working that morning, "Boże Marta, daj whisky szybko!"[33],"Co sie stalo? Wygladasz okropnie?!"[34] Marta says. Kasia also pops her head out of the kitchen, but seeing how bad the situation is she wisely decides to let me have the drink first and ask questions later. The whisky accompanies me outside with a badly rolled cigarette and a concerned Marta. "Hmmm, Czekaj"[35] Marta says when I explain what has happened through a wiązanka[36] of expletives. I visit Kasia for a refill in the time she is gone, but anticipate a long day when Marta comes outside looking whiter than me – I called my

---

32 Beetroot

33 Oh God Marta give me a whisky quickly!

34 What happened? You look awful?!

35 Wait

36 String of expletives

Babcia in Zakopane,[37] "Zosia nie jest dobrze"[38] – "You have to get rid of them." Appreciating the total hybrid of Polish and English which the girls and I now use together, I am informed that goats are likely only to grow in will power and the desire for fresh pastures which renders them incredibly strong. I return inside, shivering from the cold and realise that I cannot drive home at this point, only to find Kasia, charm cranked up to full force talking to a man with his paw around a pint of dark ale. It seems she has managed to convince this 'bear-man' that I have in my possession two incredible goats.

It is definitely time to call William. He thankfully has a half-day at work and although he sounds surprised, agrees to meet me at the pub. By the time he arrives, the scotch has taken effect and the tears are flowing. I explain what has happened through sobs and confess that I am not sure I can cope with pets who can paddle across the stream, negotiate barbed wire and release cows! "Thank goodness for that!" he exclaims –"I've had the worst month, all my time's gone to catching the goats, untangling them from their tethers and reinforcing their house! In fact, I feel they have taken over everything and I've been using the front door so I don't have to listen to their neurotic noise and see their destruction!"

The bear-man is walked over by Kasia, he knows some Christian nuns in the area who run an addiction rehabilitation centre for adults utilising animals for the process. The farmer has been phoned and will reclaim Daisy, who has hopefully not battered in the kitchen door and squashed the dogs, so we are free to jump into William's car and follow the map, drawn on a napkin to the nun's centre.

The grounds are enormous and chickens run free, pecking the dirt around our feet. It could not be better we think to ourselves. The nuns are amicable and we seize our chance. Before they have a chance to object, we are halfway home. Approximately 10% of the potato patch which William planted remains, the broccoli has been

37 Grandma, in a mountainous region of Poland

38 Zosia, it's not good

decimated and the courgettes are a urinating favourite for the dogs – still, not bad for a first attempt I think to myself, spirits high. The farmer is doing something at the fence, I go over to help him and he swears his cows are docile. Daisy is reunited with her companions and the rogue goat Horns is cornered and marched into the trailer. Little Ears is still bashing her head into the fence and trying to get out – strange creatures – always wanting to be one step further away than is possible. I walk her for the last time to the trailer. A sadness envelops us as we take the last pictures and say our goodbyes. We don't bother giving the dogs this opportunity, seeing as Caine and Blue are very much a hunting pack now and Caine likes to impress his lady with death-grip ninja moves on Horns.

The Sisters poured over us with thanks for such a generous gift, promises to feed the goats only from their organic vegetable garden and invitations to visit whenever we like. The dogs scout round at home, looking for the sergeant majors of the garden. In their absence, they roll in the grass and reclaim their territory. William and I walk hand in hand around the house several times, marvelling at the lack of manic energy and discussing the experience. In the end, we had saved animals, had a go at small-holding and dedicated them to a good cause. Clearly, we are not cut from goat-farmer-cloth and the idea of free-range chickens is put on the backburner until the advent of next year at least.

William and his son spend a couple of days dismantling the goat house and soon, all traces of their presence have faded. I sit outside with my coffee most mornings, listening to the babbling stream. My timing coincides with a neighbour it seems, an old man I have seen wondering around the vicinity barefoot, with the uncanny ability of suddenly appearing. One morning, I watch him as he turns to my gate and walks in. It is like a scene from a surreal film because I do not stir, or even manage a greeting. The dogs walk to welcome the visitor but uncharacteristically quietly (and we are talking about two fully grown Dobermans). I am puzzled when he sits down next to me on the sun-soaked bench. The man says nothing, we do not look at each other, resting in a comfortable silence. He stays until my coffee is long cold.

After a couple of days this scenario repeats itself, only this time I smile to myself and recognise how liberating it is to sit in human company without any social pleasantries or the need to maintain a stimulating conversation. I am touched by the visits and I wonder if this old man has been the deliverer of the canvas pouches which contain the sprouts I have been germinating on the window sill and sprinkling over each meal. I have absorbed something from my nutritional studies (thankfully) and sprouts help the body to produce the enzymes it needs for digestion which are more readily stimulated by raw foods.

Even if my companion is completely mad, I am touched by his visits. I wonder quietly if this is what it feels like have grandparents (having never really known mine). I imagine them as a benevolent presence, a fountain of knowledge on traditional methods of life which are being called upon to regain sustainability. This time he says "Goodbye Miss" before leaving and I look him in the eye for the first time, my eyes meet an unwavering glacial-blue piercing gaze, surrounded by wild eyebrows and a shocking-white mane of hair. His clothes look handwoven and curl at the hems, he is barefoot again and has an unshaven face. In some way he seems ageless, a facet of nature, seamlessly emerging from the elements; the dogs are almost sedated in his presence and birds dare to investigate the wild flowers in the garden at close range.

I construe wild tales in my imagination as I walk the dogs early the next day. Perhaps he is the last 'Shaman of Scotland' come down from the hills, to observe our dissociation from nature and collective fall from grace. I feel I am being observed like the fox in *The Little Prince* who teaches the Prince that wildness can be tamed a little at a time, until a need for the other develops, leading to companionship. Whilst mulling all this over, I realise that I must have become reliant on the mysterious visits, why else would I be walking the dogs at the crack of dawn each morning?!

Two mornings later my visitor returns. Just as I am relaxing into his silence, he begins to speak in a meandering tone, "I have become bored with my life," he says, I stay staring ahead of me, afraid that if I turn to him he may disappear. "I was waiting for your romance with the goats to end, you city people come out here with your grand schemes, thinking you can control nature. First my friend, you must surrender to it." Too stunned to speak I let him talk on. He has decided to help me restore my garden which the goats destroyed. Sitting quietly on the bench with my companion now chattering away like a Brazilian parrot, I am content in the knowledge that I am regaining something which I did not even know I had missed.

Although William has not yet met our guardian angel, he is pleased this presence has appeared in our lives. I am curious to see how this learning will unfold, as I bask in the comforts of home and we all wish the goats well on the next leg of their journey through life. I made a few batches of foolproof muffins, following a recipe acquired from William's mum and my companion savours them with a warm smile, looking far into horizon. He does not need to say it, I know: "It is only with the heart that one can see rightly: what is essential is invisible to the eye."[39]

39 *The Little Prince,* Antoine De Saint-Exupery

A Wish for Joy on the Journey

The wilds of Cananda

It is often said that before a couple venture into the lifelong commitment of raising children, they should first attempt dog keeping. Without consistency and commitment from the parents, those irresistibly cute angels become cheeky adolescent monkeys – a lesson William and I are quickly learning. We are model parents, scoring high in exercise levels, quality of food and love. After my Lesbos adventures, it was William's turn to pursue further steps in his development as a therapist. He was getting ready to go to Hawaii for his graduation from a 100-day programme. I was happy for William, however, over tea with my father, he noticed my sadness. Hours later he called, "Darling, I feel you need to complete your training in self-development. I hear there is a course in Hawaii...". This is the moment when a father becomes his little girl's superhero and off I went, to join my tartan-clad darling.

Being met by a towering Scotsman clutching twelve coho salmon under his arm by any airport standards is quite a scene! Having befriended a First Nations' man on the Queen Charlotte Islands, William fished these beauties out of the water within half an hour. My clever sweetheart seemed to have everything organised, very fresh fish dinner and a romantic ferry ride across the water to Vancouver Island, where I could relax into the Canadian pace of things. The plan was to drive from Vancouver to Los Angeles, via Seattle and San Francisco, fly to Hawaii for his graduation and return home. The car was a '97 blue Buick Regal purchased for the modest sum of $50 which was effectively free because it came with a full tank of gas. We swiftly christened him Benny, stuck a huge insurance cover on him in preparation for the 'sue-crazy' culture of the States and hit the road.

As we entered America by water to Port Angeles, I was reminded of the paradoxical reality in this land of super-sized proportions. On the one hand it is possible to order a vegan take-away at 3 am and yet on the other it is impossible to obtain something vaguely healthy most of the time, especially on the road. In an attempt to make everything easier, most things can be done from the comfort of your car from drive-thru bank machines to car mechanics called 'Mr. Lube', which got our British humour going. You sit in the car while your oil is changed. However, filling the car with petrol becomes a travesty if you do not have a zip-code.

There is a sense both in Canada and the USA that the land is vast and expansive, one feels dwarfed by its magnitude. Perhaps this is the reason for the enormous compound-like shops which are impossible to walk between, huge homes and enormous cars? However, these border-lands differ greatly in feel. The States feels like an unsafe environment and everything is done from the comfort of the car; models of luxury in cruising (basically extensions of the sofa), even our old Buick has many modern gimmicks. A Range Rover stands out as one of the biggest cars on the road in the UK, not so here, where everyone seems to need a pick-up truck, often placed on enormous wheels which make them look like ridiculous toys every little boy dreams of. Bigger is definitely better and many Hummers – grotesque army style jeeps can be seen on the road, which frankly, look as though only someone with a *huge* inferiority complex could justify driving around a city. William is in heaven as he delights over these fuel-guzzling monsters, "Is America recession proof? How much longer can they afford to do five-mile to the gallon?!" we wonder, not to mention the total disregard for depleting the planet's resources...

Ordering something simple is like going head-to-head with the Spanish Inquisition: "A coffee and a sandwich please," it begins; "Sure, black or white? Regular milk or soy? Which size? To go or to eat in? Which loaf...(lists ten choices)? Mayo, butter or margarine? Special, deluxe, supreme or regular size sandwich? Fries or a salad with that? Regular fries, wedges or crinkle? Vinaigrette, thousand island, Caesar, balsamic or blue cheese dressings??" It is enough to make you think twice about ordering anything!

As we make headway down Highway 101, from Seattle to Los Angeles, I imagine that living in the wilderness of America, it would be easy to become strange, bordering on mad; whereas in Canada there is a sense of loneliness. It is certainly calmer that side of the border and although many of the systems are the same, there is more sincerity in the plastic 'Have a nice day' style of the Americans. The difference between the people is clearly illustrated with a visit to Vancouver; a big city on water which is safe, calm and more harmonious in feel than any city I have ever visited. However, there is something to be said for the simplicity of the layout of American cities given that we were able to complete a 2,000 mile trip without one single map containing the entire journey! The road inspires William, "Soph, what do you think about letting the shining BMW bike loose out here on Route 66?" My look speaks a thousand (uncensored) words…

The reports from home over Skype go from bad to worse; the dogs understood the teenage 'free-house' scenario. Blue (the young temptress), proved herself a clever minx who could: open doors with her mouth; rip apart duvets, spewing fluff all over 'Grandma's' house while she was at work; eat wallpaper off the walls and forget her toilet training. On walks, Caine and Blue seemed to have contracted selective deafness. When I was in two minds about going home due to the disastrous dog situation and a complete drought in funds, a roadside diner waitress said to me, "Honey, ya gotta think like this; in ten years time which decision would ya have ratha made?" This was the clincher, I decided to stay out for a little longer (and get a loan), as we took the flight out to Hawaii, looking forward to piña coladas in the sun; a well-deserved break from the road.

We arrived into Honolulu expecting the post card dream: a woman in a grass skirt with garlands of flowers and a beachside lodge. Instead, the heat was dense and close, I felt as though I had jumped off Marlowe's boat in Conrad's *Heart of Darkness*. Daytime mosquitoes and sludge brown water – expectations are a terrible thing! Stuck in the back waters of the Hawaiian Bronx, far off the beaten track, I wonder if this is what is necessary to raise my social conscience? Anywhere you go, the world has two faces: one is for show, happy and colourful. The other is hidden, sad and full of shame. The reality of Hawaii is a fast food joint on every corner and $5 for a loaf of bread. My observations would certainly not sell dream holidays! I encountered people with very little who would offer you anything they could, whilst paradoxically wandering through neighbourhoods full of men in wife-beater vests and huge dogs gnashing their teeth at the end of chains. I will never forget a local stopping his pick-up truck to advise me that walking around in a (long) maxi-dress would get me into trouble.

There were days when we made it to pristine Hawaiian beaches which were beautiful, ate shrimps and drank cocktails. Although the overwhelming impression was of a place become America's playground, full of cheery locals, Starbucks and McDonald's, it felt more like it's dustbin. The locals, a naturally welcoming people, veil a deep unhappiness: another casualty of the white man. The Hawaiian Queen was imprisoned by the Americans, their culture and language was outlawed. They are a people disempowered; expected to be happy about the A-list owning million dollar homes and the advent of tourism as the main industry.

It is easy when one encounters Native Hawaiians, wonderful warriors and Shamans connected to the earth, to feel disgusted with our white heritage. From NativeAmericans to Indigenous Australians and New Zealand's Maoris; native peoples have been decimated and forced to live in the social gutter. When I found myself at the First Nations summit in Canada, I shared a cigarette with a woman who had eyes greener than the jungle itself. She said "All my people had these eyes before first contact." This means before the coming of the white man. Later they were all but wiped out, when they were given blankets impregnated with smallpox.

It is an awful moment when you realise that even if you have achieved an A* in your studies, you are only regurgitating the history of the victorious. These people now live on reserves which are depressing and not at all representative of their past territories. They cannot hunt or eat seasonally. The loss of old knowledge and language to a large degree has crippled them. The sham of residential schools would need an entire historical chronicle to explain function and effects. Suffice to say that each person should educate themselves in order to understand the state of the native peoples, as a result of conquerors' machinations. I remember a wonderful meeting with Aleksandra Ziółkowska-Boehm in my Kraków days when I attended a presentation of her book: *Otwarta Rana Ameryki* 'America's Open Wound', about the plight of the

Native Americans. Let's hope that the ancestral spirit returns to enough of us, to make a difference.

The Psychology of Vision seminar began. The leader had some fun with William and I, as we were the only couple there together, prodding us and finding out our 'issues'. Thankfully, we are both self-aware enough for this not to cause an uproar behind closed doors. Can you imagine standing up in front of a room full of people and announcing what you do not like about your partner while they are sitting next to you?! After the honeymoon period is over, your partner learns to drive you crazy in a matter of seconds. Everything which annoys you about them is what you have repressed in yourself and they are simply a mirror. Would you forgive yourself for being thoughtless, forgetful, grumpy etc...? The only way to deal with these things is to keep loving the person, rather than closing down.

In our case, William announced that indecisiveness was a quality he did not accept in himself, therefore my common ailment annoyed him. I on the other hand do not think of myself as an angry woman and I find his temper to be an unattractive quality. However, denying that there is an angry witch inside me is ridiculous, because something only needs to happen and I am immediately a drama queen, calling friends and family. This is 'closet' angry behaviour or passive aggression. When I look at things from this angle, I think I would prefer a short, sharp burst of anger which is over quickly, instead of a prolonged sulk. Unfortunately, a frequently used strategy of mine is burying myself under the smallest shell, at the bottom of the ocean, which my partner can never reach. The planet is entering a new paradigm and partnership is the only way to get through it, we are all being called upon to take the next step in working together in relationships, business and transnational communication.

Post-Hawaii, on the eve of our flights home, we decide that Benny – the $50 buck wonder – is too good to scrap and accept an overnight invitation with a friend of William's. An interesting Halloween evening transpires with a Shaman in L.A. We ingest some plant extracts and journey the universe, guided from one bliss bubble to the next – whether in the jungle or in a concrete metropolis – shamans certainly know how to party! For the next two days we drive for fourteen hours to hit Canada. At this point it is clear that the driving has interfered with our brain functions. We are faced with a militant female Immigration Officer at the Canadian border, just past Seattle and the simple question: "Where are you headed?" when met by our catatonic expressions and mono-syllabic replies lands us in a drug search! Following a quick check of the car which contains nothing illegal, we are let into Canada and I realise how worn down we are from the road.

We arrive somewhere along the North Thompson River in the Canadian wilderness and the similarities to home are astounding, if you can imagine pristine Scotland 100 years ago. The five-year-old girl inside chuckled long and hard at what sounded like the 'Cocacola' road, being the Coquihalla highway. Angus is William's dear friend and a wild man of the hills. Although I was forewarned about his nature, I couldn't have imagined so charming a heart. A man who dedicates his life to necessities such as chopping wood and tending his land (which includes a swamp, beaver colony, bear feeding ground and wolf through-road), whilst his girlfriend makes candles and soaps. Angus often takes his dogs and heads into the snow for a week of skiing during which time he digs a cave for shelter. An eye-opener for me was that he doesn't have huskies, his dogs are literally half-wolf. They come and lay by the fire, but have savage exchanges between themselves and are not keen for affection. They dig holes outside as their beds, but have names and come when called (most effectively when it involves food). We were taken for a walk in Wells Gray Park, which is as big as England! We watch huge waterfalls frozen in flow and most worryingly, notice big paw prints in our tracks on the way back to the car. I mention this to Angus and he estimates that a pack of eight wolves took advantage of our trail (though we novices could only see one print). Cleverly, only one wolf does the hard job of breaking through the snow and the others follow in their pawprints.

As I trudge in waist deep snow, I am filled with childlike delight for this way of life. Time has not moved here, it *is* a hundred years behind for Angus – the economic crisis has no bearing on him as he is self-sufficient. Who cares if his shower water is yellow and smells of rotten eggs, it's natural, straight from the Earth. This is the next level up from our life in the country and everyone at home thinks *we* are hippies! Are we happier accumulating material comforts? Buddha said that busyness and laziness are the two enemies of peace. I wonder what it is all *for* because the mania of doing things and accumulating objects does not add any time to our lives.

As most travellers, we come home as patriots (temporarily), tired of the car, a new motel every night and the long road each day. We are delighted and our hairy 'babies' are overjoyed to see us. William and I settle into earning some hard cash before Christmas arrives, as the trip was an unplanned budget-attack. Everyone is however warned that this one will be a modest and recycled-wrapping-paper event. Rather than making a Christmas list I will be making a list of Commandments: not to forget that the world is my mirror and a wish for joy on the journey. I have begun to see, that as in travel, so in life: the destination is not really important, it is the *getting there* that counts.

Benny the Buick

The drive-through-tree

Ben the carthorse

Free Falling

As I sit looking out at snow-capped hills, through Ladyholm's misty windows, I cannot believe how quickly the pace of life back home has enveloped me. Having spent five weeks away travelling the USA and Canada, something which struck me were the low speed limits; 40 mph in some places and people actually sticking to them! Scotland has been virtually swimming these last weeks. It is dark and I am driving at 20 mph because I cannot see a thing in front of me – the windscreen wipers are on full and the road keeps vanishing from view round the tight bends. Yet, there is still someone driving with their car as close to my posterior as possible, flashing me to go faster. Instead of speeding up slightly to minimise the glare off their headlights I think to myself – "No!" I have just returned from Hawaii and a workshop entitled 'The Restoration of Peace'. I will **not** be harassed into this crazy pace! I have to keep reinforcing this as I walk around the supermarket and even with the dogs at the Loch, there is a manic energy in the UK which infiltrates us everywhere, pushing forward all the time.

After some time I found out that our guardian angel's name is Hamish, that he used to be a man of the sea and that he does not indulge in the comfort of footwear from April to November! He laughs at our nomadic culture, flying across the globe constantly, imagining that we will meet our trueselves thousands of feet above the clouds, or in a strange land. Hopes are dashed when people dream that they will return forever altered and more capable of handling the situation at home. I fear that when we take a trip for the wrong reasons – namely trying to escape from ourselves, we return home rested, but not revitalised and the same old thought patterns quickly capture us once again. The real reason to take a trip is to enjoy every step of the way, free-falling into the universe's wise hands. Hamish cannot stop marvelling at us, he keeps saying we are uncovering part of our soul-purpose and it is shining brightly through our eyes, lending dignity and whole-heartedness to our speech. My attempts at country desserts still fail to impress him even though I experiment each time he is in the garden when 'lectures' have concluded. A 'right good crumble' is needed, so I speed over to my mother-in-law's and get the most traditional recipe she has.

One morning finds me taking the dogs for their daily circuit, a several mile jaunt around the fields surrounding our house. Here, the land works its own magic and William is temporarily abated from trying to convince me to emigrate to Canada – I am sure that he has lived a past life there as the land seems to resonate with his very cells. When he insists, I stamp my feet like a true Ślązaczka[40] and affirm that I'm not leaving my beloved Mama, Dad, Scotland and Poland (only a short flight away.) I also know that no matter how far William could bend Mama's ear, her might could set Cerberus free at the serious proposal of such an idea.

All of a sudden, my reverie is broken – a BMW is swerving all over the road, racing towards me and I am wondering if my time is up – if I will have a life-review, see the white light and hear THE VOICE. I immediately think of my loved ones and the last things I said to them which is why I absolutely detest leaving things badly when it is over something small, imagine that the last spoken words were: "Fine!" "Whatever!" or "I don't care." Not exactly poetic, and yes, I realise that it might have been "Don't forget to buy the milk," but I would prefer that a million times.

When I think about the death part I am mainly curious about the experience. I feel that I could leave the planet satisfied that I had known true love, made friends closer than family and thoroughly enjoyed the hybrid blood tribes I was born to. However, when I think of my family, I have to put the brakes on because this is not

40 A girl from the Silesian region in Poland where my family originate from

my time. I know it is too soon... The car screeches to a halt and a man jumps out, I recognise him as the usually soft spoken neighbour who maintains the wood paths. He looks mildly ridiculous, sporting a long waterproof trench coat, a thick band worn around the ears (always reminding me of Austrian women on skiing holidays) and he is so agitated that before he even begins speaking, he is jumping up and down. He is shorter than I am but for the length of this exchange I am unconscious of the fact. "Where is your other dog?" he screams as he comes closer to my face. I am standing with Caine by my side on a lead and I last saw Blue tearing through the trees a few minutes prior (a common occurrence seeing as she is a two year old Doberman who likes to run). I note his bloodshot eyes and the globules of saliva gathering at the corners of his mouth. "Yes, you don't know where it is because it has just killed one of my chickens. I've a shotgun and I am tempted to use it", at this point I am thinking he may mean on me as I look down and realise it's in his hand. The man is hysterical as he declares that he will spread the word among the neighbours – if our dogs are ever seen off the lead they are to be shot dead whether accompanied or not. I wish that Caine would bite the man's arm off and fight the urge to cry. He will not listen to anything I have to say, managing to shout some other unpleasant things at me before he jumps into his car with the shotgun and drives off screeching.

It seems that whether you live on the banks of the North Thompson River in Canada or in a tiny hamlet in Scotland, your dog can be shot by your neighbour. An unfortunate event which befell William's friend Angus the Wildman shortly after we arrived back. One of his wolf dogs was shot dead on his neighbour's property for chasing deer which happened to be on their land. This single event has shattered Angus' belief in the benevolence of the human heart, challenged his relationship with his long-term girlfriend (as the dogs are the children they never had) and destroyed his paradise. The neighbours now have a dog of their own and it would be interesting to see their reactions if Angus took a gun to it next time it went after a bear on the riverbank (on his land). Not that this issue is about vengeance, which would not solve anything, it is simply recognising that so violent an act *must* spell disaster for neighbourly relations.

If a dog is violent to humans, it would be prudent to destroy it, but if all we are talking about are some ordinary chickens, then surely an agreement between the people responsible can be reached? My dog killed your chicken, fine, I shall buy you a new one and pay for the dead one. If you ever see my dog on your land again it shall be muzzled. Feel free to catch it and drag it home, alternatively you can shoot it in the leg with a shotgun shell full of rock salt which will certainly deter it from ever coming back and if you are still not happy then you can also shoot yourself with it for kicks, I hear it packs a mean sting!!!

What we are really missing is the old way. William often talks about his Grandfather's antics, he was a gamekeeper and repository for the wisdom we are losing and fast. When you purchased a dog in the countryside, you would ask the farmer if you could borrow one of his rams and put the puppy in a pen with it, the ram would charge a few times (without harming it) to scare the dog off farm animals for life. Alternatively, if a dog killed a chicken you would tie the dead chicken to its head for the whole day. These days, in our mania for personifying animals we are becoming rather foolish, sometimes the way it's always been deserves a second thought.

It is much easier to intimidate a woman with a shotgun than a 6'3 Scotsman. However, after the visit William paid the neighbour, I do not think he will be in a rush to do this again! I heard William ask him if he had a daughter, affirmative, "Would you want someone to talk to her the way you spoke to my girlfriend?" He could not agree. After this, the trees themselves were bending backwards not to hear the rest of the exchange. William returned proud of himself (I was too), he handled it. We'll buy the neighbour some chickens and he'll never come anywhere near me again with the shotgun. Problem solved.

Old Hamish says "Eh, people will be people. They haven't farmed this land for centuries they bought it with their 'guilty' gentry money, so they feel they must protect it. It is from this need to defend that all the evils from the world spring forth." This is a beautiful philosophical thought, but it does not help us in this moment of panic when we begin to feel imprisoned by our home, no longer cradled by the surrounding area and I notice that both of us have become quietly fanatical about locking the doors.

Blue has been re-Christened the 'Stealth Assassin' on account of her new muzzle which she wears at all times and these days we drive the few miles to the Loch where the dogs run carefree. Although she is prevented from causing any harm to animals, the Assassin is simply too good at what she does; yesterday, William and I witnessed her playing with something in the grass. It was a rabbit which had ventured out into the open space – between her muzzled nose and foot, Blue was stalling it. Suddenly, the direction of the wind changed and Caine came bounding over like a bear after the honey pot. He pushed Blue out of the way and administered the kiss of death. We can now see that Caine is overjoyed with Blue as things have got even better – before there was only sharing the catch, now there is the whole package plus delivery! Clearly this is something we will need to distract from in the future, I am however left thinking that if we are ever starving, our dogs could definitely hunt for us.

My dear father gave himself the job of founding a course centre, employing local people and creating an optimum environment for personal growth. He jokes that like Victor Frankenstein, his monster will ultimately consume him. The financial crisis hits its apex and I cannot allow for that, the place and the vision are too special. I rush down there (two hours away), with my fresh if relatively useless university energy to help from Tuesday to Thursday each week. My job is to learn everything. When I have mastered the work of four people, I am to become dad's personal assistant for the next six months. My father is something of a technological dinosaur and his is the only desk in the office which exhibits piles of papers rather than a computer! The time has come to work off the financial deficit I have been for the last twenty-four years and I have to say, I am looking forward to getting to know the business side of 'Pops'.

The rebounder

A campaign launched at the local stables saw Ben the cart-horse about to be sold. He is known in the industry as being 'bomb proof' – as solid as a house. Here we see that it is never too late for a parent to try and fulfil the wishes of their children. My favourite weekends as a girl were spent riding with my Dad and I always dreamed of having my own horse, however, when this proved impossible I moved on and began enjoying inner city life as a teen. Dad has obviously never forgiven himself for the pony dream and at his suggestion I took some riding lessons with Ben. Here emerged a triumvirate – after singing Ben's praises to me, both dad and his secretary inadvertently also fell for him. And so, the three of us became proud horse owners, we have never yet decided who owns which part! Ben has added some spring (and stretch) to our lives. Post-lessons see us walking like John Wayne as he is as wide as a sofa, but I think to myself, it is definitely worth it. Petroleum is fast dwindling, electric cars are not yet accessible and a horse is an economically viable method of transport!

The lease on our house will run out soon and the year-long experiment with it. I am wondering what William is thinking, constantly second-guessing his looks (which I am sure is driving him crazy). However, I cannot shake the feeling of dread which rears its ugly head every now and then, making me wince when I recall the two occasions when he intimated that we may not be in this house for much longer. There was a definite assertion of independence in the statements and I feel suddenly as though the game is up. The referee has blown the whistle and pulled the red card – this whole experience has been too magical, too full of bathos; moving seamlessly between the sublime and the ridiculous daily. No, these kinds of things do not happen and girls from London do not fall for Scottish men and set up a rural life, as though by accident. I am reminded of a quote from one of my favourite films – *Withnail and I,* by the main character: "We've gone on holiday by mistake", provided as an explanation for the ridiculous situations which transpire. So too, I feel I could explain all the laughs and the more serious casualties, namely the chickens, if anyone cared to ask. Neither of us are raised farmers and we do not intend to become deadly serious and morose about the whole business of animal keeping and tending the land.

I find with some surprise that phrases such as "a wee bit" seem to be slipping out of my mouth all the time, however, they sound very much like an English girl speaking Scottish words. They do not roll off the tongue the way they do when pronounced by a true inhabitant of these lands. When William speaks in his really thick accent, the richness of the 'r's and the 'o's swirl around my head and I no longer seek a sense in the words. Quite forgetting where one ends and another begins I feel as though I am overhearing a conversation carried on the wind, between the hills, the mossy grass and the trees. I adore the way that the Scots refer to 'the now' as though it were a concrete time which exists in every moment. The power of 'the now' may have been a more encouraging title of Eckhardt Tolle's *The Power of Now*!

We decide not to travel anywhere over the festive season on account of our ailing budget and my decision that cheap travel no longer exists. Once all the airport taxes have been added and you have been charged for everything they can imagine from check-in baggage, every *tiny* kilo overweight, headphones and blankets – a satisfying price is a rare pleasure. In addition, any relaxation from the holiday is undone at the airport on the way home, after waiting in a queue like a cow at market. I am always promising myself I will not fly long-haul again until I have saved the money to do so in comfort. Perhaps, I shall renew this one on my Resolution List and the New Year will find me sipping champagne from tulip-shaped glasses while a handsome steward reads me the options for dinner!

I'll Be Home for Christmas

Winter wonderland

When I think of Christmas, I am transported to being pulled along in a sledge by fourteen huskies, all foaming at the mouth whilst swaddled in furs and getting whisked off from Kiruna airport. The only thing I knew was that my dad and my stepmother were nearby and I could see some lights dancing in the sky – the Aurora Borealis or Northern Lights took my breath away. The Ice Hotel suddenly appeared; sculpted entirely from ice complete with bar, glasses, chandeliers, staircases and bed slabs. It is re-carved each winter.

Parallel to this recollection, I can hear my Wujek[41] Boguś causing uproar; staggering around with a bottle of Wyborowa[42] under one arm and a saw in the other, singing. William is not spared this tradition; in our town, the men marked out a tree for chopping under the cover of darkness. They would often have a few stiff drinks for encouragement, being at serious minus numbers outside. This would get them to the tree, perhaps even to chopping it down. They would however rarely make it back to the house. The women found themselves sitting at home with the decorations ready and waiting with no man and no tree for the night. The morning would find half-frozen husbands and brothers stumbling around for their loot. William enlisted a friend for the job as I, according to tradition, sat waiting at home.

Around 10 pm, there are some scraping noises at the door. I rush out to see William and his friend stumbling under the weight of an enormous tree, branches waving everywhere – "Darling, this is a lot bigger than the one we picked isn't it?" I ask, wondering how on earth we are going to get it through the door, never mind into a room. "Aye, I've brought you the most beautiful tree in Scotland! As the two of them stagger around I retreat into the warm. Typical men I think to myself, bigger is *not* always better! We are still trying to cut back one end of the tree to get it standing in the hallway.

This year, I shall be host for the first time. I have experienced three different Christmas traditions thanks to my English father, Polish mother and Swedish stepmother (in Sweden they are called bonus-mothers and bonus-children, terms we both prefer). It is a wonderful way of skipping the negativity of the 'evil stepmother' and bringing some joy to the idea of *winning* another person to love in your life. I shall have the pleasure of experiencing all the traditions this year. A Polish Wigilia[43] and introduction to our traditions for William will begin the festivities; the reins will

---

41 Uncle

42 Famous Polish vodka

43 Christmas Eve, the main celebration in Poland

be handed to Iona, William's mum for Christmas Day lunch and Boxing day will see us driving to my Dad's for a Swedish lunch. It is truly the best of three worlds.

The Swedes like us Poles love herrings, smoked fish and a stiff drink. Christmas Eve finds them sipping glögg (mulled wine with a healthy dose of brandy), schnapps, washed down with beer and a Swedish version of coca-cola. A small glass of each is poured and you drink from each one periodically after a song. My bonus-mum sees one of the more poignant differences in these traditions as: the Swedes have to sing a song before a drink and the Brits only sing after too many! This usually bodes for a merry time especially since the food is served smorgasbord style, which involves standing up frequently (no chance of hiding any swaying!).

Our Polish Wigilia is a rich evening full of tradition. Everyone helps to decorate the tree with bompki[44]. Inevitably my Ciocia Irminka does all the cooking (on account of her supreme skill). Something which always stands out in my memory is the carp served on the Wigilijny Stół[45]; it is not amongst my favourite sea food with a pungent taste and many bones, however, it is a mass-slaughter across Poland. For about two days these sizeable fish have been swimming around the bathtub, looking at you as you brush your teeth. The afternoon before the big day finds my uncle brooding over a bottle of vodka. The next day the carp are miraculously presented as battered pan-fried cutlets and in aspic. Many people do not like the taste, but tradition persists even though you never feel quite the same about a relaxing bath again! We gather at the table when the first star shows in the sky. A prayer is said, over a glass of something and it is opłatek[46] time. As we share a piece of opłatek with everyone present, we take a minute to appreciate them; often verbalising things we have not found time to say in the course of the year. Each person has a piece and when

44 Baubles

45 Christmas table

46 Rice bread which is broken before eating

you share with the other, you break off some of theirs. It is fundamental that everyone shares with each guest.

There should be some straw under the tablecloth and twelve very different dishes. An empty space is reserved for a lost traveller or the homeless. A wonderful gesture, but in this day and age, no one realistically lets anyone into their homes. Excuse my cynicism, but they would perhaps be frisked first!

As I write this, I realise how much ceremony and ritual there is in our Polish way. For the Brits, Christmas Day is the apex of the festivities commencing with stockings, big presents and a champagne breakfast to gently ease the five hour wait for the turkey as I remember! The table presents: a bird, bread sauce, mince pies, puddings and all kinds of alcohol, not forgetting the childhood nemesis of boiled Brussels sprouts. Some families spread their gifts through the day, leaving something to look forward to. A resurfacing tradition from the deep past involves stuffing the turkey with a duck, which contains a grouse and cooking them all together, inside one another.

A pre-Christmas get together sees my girlfriends from university all gathered together in Leeds. Anna has just moved into a flat with her boyfriend and is proudly nesting. Assembled from all over the country, we make the last pilgrimage before the festivities. I am immediately pestered for Polish vodka and Vogue cigarettes, Becky for Sing Star – the karaoke you can actually lose at and Hannah is helped with her bags, containing pots of ready cooked delights. One thing is for sure, we may still behave like students when we get together, but thanks to Hannah; we eat like kings.

The girls are particularly attached to Zoladkowa Gorzka[47] and Kraków owing to our post-graduation week there, when we revelled in our new-found freedom and each other's company. However, I would not let the visit pass without showing off the motherland. We climbed up to Morskie Oko[48], huffing and puff-

47 A special type of Polish vodka which is excellent for the stomach (in moderation of course)

48 A glacial lake in the Zakopane region in Poland

ing, passing the Górale[49] with their horse-drawn waggons – I wasn't going to let them have it easy! At the summit, there were those who continued the short but vertical climb up to Czarny Staw[50] and those who waited over a pint of piwo z sokiem [51]– who shall not be named!

These meetings are invaluable to us. As young women who love each other we explore the different experiences we are having in relationships, work, study and emotional states. With every year I treasure the sharing more and more; lessons from our peers are easier to assimilate than from our elders. People often say that the friends one makes at university are special, I do believe this is true; when else in your life do you make friends so close they know your bra size, how you take your tea, what kind of hangovers you have, how you deal with break-ups and the style of your essay writing?! With time I also value the student luxury of being bored together. These girls are family to me (an amusing, often slightly inebriated one!) We now number amongst us: two lawyers, a primary school teacher, a *nearly* architect, a property manager, an artist and a journalist – not bad for a bunch of scruffs!

Kraków has gifted me with such wonderful moments. It is now a complete patchwork of different people and experiences. I remember the euphoria of graduating from university with all my friends and 'The Snobs'. The motherland will never leave me, ensuring the health of our customs wherever I go on the planet. My darling friend Ania has been in Łódź, finalising her wedding plans. Our 'Snob' club has stood the test of time and distance. At the time of our reunion in 2010 it will have been two years since our paths separated, which fills me with optimism for the future. Ania is on her next step in womanhood. She wants a proper Polish

49 People from the Polish mountains

50 Another even more pristine glacial lake just above Morskie Oko

51 Lager served with either ginger or raspberry-flavoured syrup and often drunk with a straw

wedding and 'The Snobs' are in charge of the bramy [52] – I predict some serious vodka drinking and potato peeling challenges!

My dear Hamish has invited himself to our Christmas proceedings, although he is rather vague with dates and times, I presume he will arrive when he is hungry and I will pretend that everything is made by my precious hands due to his disdain for processed foods. Despite the fact that he is inconvenienced by having to wear shoes in winter, it is his season, the frosty mornings suit his white, bushy-beard and eyebrows – our very own eccentric Father Christmas!

This time of year courts reflection and a desire to tie up loose ends; a chance to look back at the year and see what we have achieved. It has certainly been a dynamic year: I have tried my hand at country life and committed myself seriously to a man, a land and dogs. The decision to do this has impacted my emotional health dramatically after a lifetime of gypsy-hood. It is time to go forth, love one another and depending on how rebellious one is, to make a list of resolutions or sins to commit... go ahead, take some risks!

Wesołych Świąt and Merry Christmas!

---

52 A custom which involves people obstructing the newlyweds from leaving. They often have to do tasks such as peeling potatoes or chopping logs which prepares them to work as a team in the first challenges of married life

Looking Into the Crystal Ball

Someone throwing some 'baggage' into the bonfire at Biggar

As the New Year chimes in, I think about people merrymaking all over the globe. No doubt there are people jumping into hot geysers in Iceland and Finns dipping in ice-holes. Thankfully, the locals of Biggar wrap up warm and offer their obsessions and neuroses for vaporisation into the ether. There are no fireworks, only the almighty blaze as tall as a building, which keeps everyone warm: teenagers, the elderly, young children and police enjoy the night together. Scottish bagpipe music blasts out of every pub and merrymakers show off their moves waiting for midnight when everyone surrenders their unwanted 'baggage' to the blaze.

I watch as one woman struggles forward with a beautiful leather Louis Vuitton suitcase and a box of pictures, throwing them with difficulty into the blaze. Pity about the case I think to myself, perhaps she was disposing of a lover's memories. I catch a glimpse of a man at the other side of the fire, throwing in empty boxes of crisps and biscuits – we all understand that feeling – to enter the New Year without cravings, what a luxury! I wonder if we comprehend the layers which find us all addicts; beneath food, drugs and sex lay the subtler addictions: thought patterns, emotions and endorphins. Some have scrubbed themselves clean for the New Year, others wait with heavily bearded smiles, a contingent carry presents as an offering for 2010 and a few shamanic-trance dance their way into it. In whatever way we seek to bribe or win the favour of the New Year, we all hope it will be better than the last.

Thankfully, William and I were wise enough to fill the house with supplies; the cars were completely snowed-in for a fortnight! Mama and I introduced William's family to the tradition of opłatek before eating Christmas Lunch. Everyone was touched and there were tears flowing as we sat down. I think this is one of our more beautiful traditions and I am sure they will always remember it, perhaps even adopting it into their annual ritual. On New Year's Day, Mama and I were introduced to a Scottish custom. William was tearing round the house shouting something about "First-footers"; when you are the first people over the threshold in the New Year, you offer a piece of coal which represents warmth and a carrot to the person you are visiting. In our village in the South of Poland, we give people a candle to light their way in the coming twelve months. Over William's mum Iona's hearty steak pie, we all reminisce and talk of our plans for the future. I rather like this tradition of gathering the family after the partying (or not) of the night before, to regroup and face the next year together.

As I began preparations for my 25th year which commenced on the 2nd of January, I decided to start with this season's buzz-word; 'detox'. Detoxification or garbage disposal can occur in more ways than one; physical, emotional and psychological. That morning saw me frantically cleaning the house and feng-shui-ing my mind and wardrobe! I did not want to meet my birthday with too much junk!

Drastic and often unrealistic resolutions seem to be out of favour; perhaps the reality of our economic situation has shocked us into living within our means. Many friends greeted the New Year in a low key fashion, quietly at home with their families. A couple of girlfriends channelled more of the Bridget Jones spirit, happily eating ice-cream in their pyjamas. Seeing as this one was a quiet affair, Mama and I decided to call everyone who would really appreciate the thought. I talked to young women my age scattered across the globe and many were envious of my 'settled' position in my relationship; the single state seemed to be a widespread cause of depression. Their mothers shared a worryingly limited dream: they implied that having a partner was the ultimate goal, as they were craving grandchildren. My personal words of warning: children are *not* an extension of our successes or failures; neither are they an antidote for our loneliness. I am surprised because the majority of my single friends have *chosen* some time off from the rollercoaster of relationships, enjoying freedom. The hysterical approach I fear, will not only scare away potential suitors, it also makes one miserable company and is certainly a questionable approach in courting the New Year.

In a chilly -19.5^0 in Scotland, I watch as people are stranded, abandoning their cars, trains are cancelled, air travel is near impossible, hundreds of schools are empty and roads are closed. The country has broken down in the worst winter for thrity years;

it is colder than in my freezer! I feel proud of my motherland; in Poland the temperatures dance below freezing for the entirety of winter and people still go to work, use public transport, children go to school and everyone knows to stock up well with coal over winter otherwise they will freeze! We learnt this the hard way; lesson number one – never start making a fire when you have not got enough wood or coal inside the house; going out when you are glowing is awful! However, with the heating oil gone, a week to wait and wood leaving our shed fast, we may soon be hacking up furniture to keep us warm! On a record night it reached -27^{0}, and William and I were still cold even with each other, cashmere bed socks (always an appreciated present), the electric blanket Mama gifted us for Christmas and two huge dogs!

As the recession takes its toll, high flying career women are suddenly finding themselves in a close embrace with domesticity; the once shunned roles of housewives and mothers are being rediscovered. The world analysts are looking into their crystal balls to predict our economic future. As we collectively rise from the ashes, open hearts and minds are at a premium. We must begin to invest in emotions, relationships and love, rather than material possessions. Even the spiritual can become waylaid; on one of my travels to India, I was told a story about a guru when he was still a young student. His father was dying as he sat meditating, adorned in beads and his teacher told him: "If human life is a school, you are avoiding the curriculum! Go and be with your father!" From the statistics, these times of hardship are not exactly pushing us to tie the knot with rates plummeting to an all time low since records began in 1862.[53]

For those who are brave enough to make the vows, a break from tradition is on the rise: Vera Wang unveiled a black wedding dress as bolder colours are now being worn for the 'big day'. The classic white dress symbolising a maiden's purity gained popularity when Queen Victoria married Prince Albert in 1840. Until this time,

---

53 Office for National Statistics: <http://www.statistics.gov.uk/pdfdir/marr0209.pdf>

women had simply worn their best dress; white and cream not being easy to clean meant brides were a colourful breed. It seems that tradition is being abandoned on account of financial and fashion statements; brides desire dresses that can be worn again and evening weddings where the bride marries and celebrates in an elegant gown to conserve finances are on the rise. With the average UK wedding setting one back approximately £20,000, it is no surprise.

We find ourselves one step closer to the controversial 2012 – a couple of years ago it was the domain of the spiritual and the conspiracy theorists – now it has passed into the popular lexicon. Everything from Mayan prophecies, web-bot projects, Hollywood movies and magnetic pole reversals are pointing to some kind of cataclysm. Some are calling it a shift in consciousness; or the next step in our evolution.

Ancient Mayan civilisations dedicated themselves to the art of predicting the future using astrology and time-keeping. They predicted the End Times in 2012. We may face elimination by our beloved planet which we are destroying, or be forced into the collapse of our speculative financial system –the figurative jugular of our world. Perhaps only something so extreme, affecting each of us could force change.

The imminent release of the Hollywood movie *2012* will no doubt dramatise these prophecies to terrifying heights. *2012* will surely become another one of Hollywood's displays, flexing their special effect muscles, only to hang it up alongside zombies and vampires when the commotion dies down. At university, I avidly read fantasy and I studied the periods in history when sci-fi and fantasy gained popularity. We find a mainstream interest in these genres when reality becomes bleak and unmanageable; it is a reflection of our subconscious. Sci-fi is 'the literature of change' and fantasy is the 'literature of longing'. Fantasy usually closes with the 'reestablishment of order', whereas sci-fi climaxes with 'the evolution to a higher order', exposing what we really crave as a society.[54] If time is a river, we can never step twice into any one part of it; the New Year is a powerful time on the planet when global energy is pushing for a new path, a time to create a new experience for ourselves.

Let us not propagate the hypnosis, disempowering ourselves into stagnation, because things are irreversible and one cannot possibly combat such a snow-balling force as climate change or political chess. We can, and do, have the power within our psyches to move mountains. Simply sitting at home or walking outside whilst generating positive thoughts will send out vibrations, attracting better things into your life and give the planet something of a feedback forum! The planet needs happy feet walking on it.

The Mighty Matterhorn Mountain

54 Treitel, <http://web.utk.edu/~wrobinso/590_lec_fan.html>

How to Beat the Winter Blues

My Uncle and I

The apocalyptic prophecies of the ancient Mayans have had an unexpected effect on travel. If the world is going to end in 2012, then the time for seeing it is now! As the people of the UK deal with the new face of the land revealed by the exiting snow, which is muddy and grey and a recession which shows no sign of lifting, holidays have moved from being a luxury to a necessity. The logic of using these apocalyptic tales as a marketing tool overwhelms me, but Thomson and First Choice Travel are encouraging us to book a break using this strategy. In these credit crunch times, we would prefer to sacrifice a new home appliance or car in favour of a getaway. In fact, a recent report showed that four out of five people were not changing their holiday plans because of the recession; however, package holidays are experiencing a boost as we hunt for value for money.

A blast of sun is a sensible investment if we are to avoid Seasonal Affective Disorder, or S.A.D. which affects an estimated half a million people per year between September and April. A lack of the sun's rays can lead to a deficiency of vitamin D and serotonin which regulates sleeping patterns, appetite and even libido. It is not surprising then, that Brits crave foreign climates to keep depression at bay. It is perhaps also why we can be seen stripping off the second a ray of sunshine appears in the sky! Our pagan ancestors practised the art of balance, worshipping each element and recognising its importance, with sun and water receiving special dues as the givers of life.

As a child I remember that the yearly or biennial family calendar was well planned once I was old enough to participate. Winters were broken up with a skiing trip in Europe, Easters were spent in Florida visiting our family in America and soaking up the sun and summers were spent in Poland. Being included in Mama's mid-Winter 'spa' trip was exciting, though it sounds more luxurious than it was.

Polish sanatoriums are available to everyone at affordable prices and still seem to have far more advanced systems for wellness than many over-priced alternatives. The concept of them is unique, the state subsidises a three week stay for each citizen every two years, where prevention of illness is the focus. Nothing can beat places like Ustrón and Busko Zdrój and their most advanced treatment in rejuvenation called cryo-therapy which involves standing in a freezing chamber in temperatures of -120° for 3-5 minutes, clad in a swim suit, thick gloves, a headband and wooden clogs. Some sanatoriums have their own healing waters and sources of mineral mud called *borowina* in which you can bathe or be wrapped. At the other end of the relaxation scale is the most extreme treatment which is used in psychiatric wards and prisons; it is needless to say, anything but pleasant. After stripping down, you cling to large metal handles at one end of a tiled room, while at the other end, the executor blasts your body with both hot and cold water jets under extremely high pressure. Funny that it's called bicze szkockie[55], when no Scot I know has ever heard of it. Apparently it is said that the reason for the name comes from the stereotype of the Scots of being slow to put their hands in their pockets and so the therapy uses both cold and hot jets to save on the water bill![56] These sanatoriums encapsulate the spirit of elderly Polish people; despite aching limbs, shortness of breath, artificial joints and Zimmer frames, they can still be found at the post-dinner tea dance enjoying innocent romances.

I prefer to worship my health and body in a Polish sanatorium, than subject myself to the questionable luxury of more glamorous spas where beautiful people pamper themselves with rose petals in the bath tub, hot-stone massages and chocolate body wraps. However, I recognise that these places have their function; if our body is our temple, then we need to find a place to nurture it. When you are living life on fast-forward it can be difficult to hit the pause button. The holistic world shouts about the evils of stress: holidays help, but to really unwind we need to turn off our phones and laptops and pamper ourselves, with whatever works.

As I reach into my memory of skiing holidays, the habit of hitting the slopes in winter was born on a childhood trip to the Austrian Kitzbühel resort. The trip was under the spiritual guidance of Ksiadz Kukla[57] and the venue, none other than a local monastery. Needless to say, our troop of Polish mothers and children did not sample the fashionable après ski bars and nightlife spots! We began and ended each day in a small chapel with a prayer. The mornings proceeded with drinking spoonfulls of 'Amol'[58] with sugar (under duress) and the

55 Hydrotherapy with water jets

56 http://regeneracja.poradnikzdrowie.pl/rehabilitacja/bicze-szkockie-metoda-wskazania-dzialanie_44200.html

57 Priest/Father

58 A herbal remedy for all ills, loved by Polish mothers for more than a 100 years

joys of ski school absorbed and exhausted us well into the afternoon. I remember the homely atmosphere and joy of sharing the evening meal, accompanied by endless cups of tea and a sense of belonging created by Father Kukla. He was not only much loved by us, but also admired as an accomplished skier.

Since I had no intention of showing off my 'Christmas' hips in Barbados (or even Tenerife) this year; I slipped my feet into fur-lined moon-boots, put on a Russian hat, Killy stirrup pants and leather-trimmed white sunglasses. Just add lip-gloss and attitude, I thought, even doing a snow-plough will look sensational (I wish!) In response to the question: 'Are you a good skier?' I must admit that what I lack in technique, I make up for in enthusiasm and brute force. I decided to reconnect with my passion for the Italian and Swiss Alps. What could be better than standing at the top of the Mighty Matterhorn 4, 500 metres above sea level, wondering how on earth I will negotiate the descent, high on adrenaline and lungfuls of pure air?! Exhilarated, dizzy and trembling with fear from the downhill run, this is where I feel most alive and truly humbled by Mother Nature. The promise of a hot meal sustains me on the descent – forget cordon bleu and nouvelle cuisine, Italy is all about mountain basics. Italy, I salute your celebration of carbohydrates! Trattorias are packed with people feasting on pizza and pasta, twirling spaghetti around their forks and sipping prosecco absolutely guilt-free! Although no one ever talks about diets on skiing holidays, the physical exhaustion, oxygenation of the brain and renewal of the cells always promotes a sense of health and well-being lasting well into the year.

As the financial storm in Britain worsens, the mass exodus of city high flyers increases as they seek refuge in the tax-free oases of the Swiss mountains. Let's hope the 'hard-done by' bankers do not cause a perennial avalanche with their insatiable appetite for glitz and cash. When we start to see stocks and shares, pounds and euros marked in the snow, we'll know it is time to hang up our skis for good and head for the beach. As usual, money talks, but do we need that noise in the silence of the snow-capped mountains?

A Lesson in Love from Hamish

Caine and Blue

'Love' is defined as 'an intense feeling of deep affection for someone' in the Oxford Concise English dictionary. Something about this multifaceted emotional state makes us all crave to be in it or be the object of it. As young girls on lunch breaks, we used to sit on the grass, pulling out the petals of daisies: 'Does he love me, does he not?' If we didn't like the answer we simply started on the next one. If only the whole business of love were as simple as plucking daisies! If you live in India or the Middle Eastern countries, you will not be celebrating Valentine's Day, because it has been banned by the authorities for sexual and Christian overtones.

The Scots are a romantic bunch at heart and traditional Valentine's celebrations were rather grand. An equal number of males and females would attend a party; all names would go into a hat, to be drawn in pairs. The couple chosen together would be each other's companion for a night of dancing and an exchange of gifts.[59] In Japan, as a boyfriend or husband, you can expect home-made chocolate from the special ladies in your life, showing your appreciation on March 14th when men give women presents. Young Korean singles can be seen gathered together on April 14, 'Black Day' sharing the black Jajangmyeon dish which gives the day its name.[60]

On the subject of matrimony, tradition dictates that a woman can ask a man to marry her on February 29th, which occurs every four years. This practice is said to have originated in 5th century Ireland, when St Bridget complained to St Patrick about women's extensive waiting for a man to propose. Once again we find the Scots to be romantic of heart, as in 1288 a law was supposedly passed allowing women to propose. It details that if the man should decline, he must pay a fine; ranging between a kiss, a silk dress or a pair of gloves for the heartbroken maiden.[61] Who said the law is devoid of feeling? Or humour for that matter; if you did not show up in the Liverpool courts, you can be expecting a poem from the Metropolitan Police: 'Roses are red, violets are blue, you've got a **warrant** and we'd love to see you'![62]

As a girl, Mama always used to write me cards with a little chocolate enclosed. Every Valentine's Day, whether in a relationship or single, we focus on the concept of universal love. It is too easy for us to be seduced by 'Hallmark holidays' and think that this day actually symbolises what card companies say – 'If he didn't get you flowers then he doesn't love you'. Come on, there are 365 days in the year when he can buy you flowers, take you for dinner and tell

---

59 <http://cultural-anthropology.suite101.com/article.cfm/valentines-day-traditions-from-around-the-world>

60 <http://www.novareinna.com/festive/valworld.html>

61 <http://marriage.about.com/cs/holidays/a/leapyear.htm>

62 <http://www.bbc.co.uk/worldservice/learningenglish/language/newsaboutbritain/2009/02/090210_nab_valentine.shtml>

you he loves you! Do not misunderstand me – I am NOT making a case against roses and chocolate! I am simply a girl, afraid that the whole scenario will pass me by as I sit on my 'worry bench', wearing my good-luck orange beret and tons of anxiety whilst puffing on my rolled cigarette!

I hear the gate lightly knock as it is pushed back into place. Since the dogs have not stopped the intruder, it must a friend. Hamish soundlessly greets them and sits next to me on my bench. No words are needed to convey my emotional state. "I just don't see the point of the emotional rollercoaster of relationships, it's so hard, how do people do it?" I explode. Silence descends as if I had not spoken and when Hamish speaks his voice sounds remote: "The path of true love is long and steep, so you had better get yourself some good shoes my girl." I can't help but laugh at this as my eyes go straight to Hamish's feet; barely covered by his home-made leather moccasins. So begins my first formal lesson in love:

"In our culture people are starved of love. We watch endless films about happy and unhappy love, we listen to hundreds of trashy songs about it – yet hardly anyone thinks that there is anything to be learned about *loving.* Most people see the problem as one of *being* loved, rather than of one's capacity to love. We aim to make ourselves 'loveable'; by being popular, wealthy and having sex appeal. Just as living is an art, so is loving; we must proceed in the discipline as with any other such as music or carpentry. Despite the deep longing for love we all have, most people fail because almost everything else is considered more important than the art: success and so on. This practice requires discipline, concentration, patience, faith, courage, the ability to take risks and readiness to accept pain and disappointment."

With an air of authority, Hamish leaves the bench and traverses the hall; pinning some scraps of paper to it – here we go, I thought he's turning preacher! Completely unfazed by my hostile attitude, Hamish pointed, as if a lecturer in an auditorium; packed to the brim with eager ears; "In the Book of Jonah, God explains that the essence of love is labour; the two are inseparable." The second battered piece of yellowed paper held the words of Saint-Exupéry's

Fox to the Little Prince: "It is the time you lavished on your rose that makes it so important"; if she doesn't get the biblical one, she will get the modern parable – I am sure Hamish thought. Crafty old goat![63]

He finished his lecture and disappeared; it worked for the Little Prince, but how am I going to translate that into the fast and often thoughtless pace of everyday life? I am thrown into thinking about the writings of Khalil Gibran; 'Even as love crowns you so shall he crucify you'; 'Even as he is for your growth so is he for your pruning'.[64] Is love synonymous with pain? The beautiful rose, our symbol of affection was born of Aphrodite's woe when her tears mingled with blood from her lover's wound.

Gone is the old University ethos: the 'anti-Valentine' party, which was all about friends and nothing to do with couples or singles. We reasoned that on Valentine's, you are likely to end up sitting at a tiny table in between two other couples, having to listen to their conversations while paying double for your dinner just because it's Valentine's Day.

I caught the end of an old *Sex and the City* episode the other night and found myself completely disillusioned – Samantha went from outrageous to pathetic and the pursuit of love through sex could be dismissed by nursery school children nowadays; "It's not gonna work, even if you are decked out in Jimmy Choos or Manolo Blahniks!" Was it a fanciful escape into such frivolities that made the show appealing, or do we simply live in a grittier reality now with forensic shows like *Crime Scene Investigation* as the champions of the channels?

Hamish returns and plucks me from my maelstrom of thoughts, by presenting me with a bunch of twigs and mossy grasses. "Burn these inside, they protect well against damp, you've some in the house." I am distracted but he regains my attention with the second bundle; a leaf with something inside, tied in a ball with

---

63 Antoine de Saint-Exupéry, The Little Prince (Wordsworth Editions Limited: 1995), p. 82

64 Khalil Gibran, The Prophet (1923) <http://en.wikiquote.org/wiki/The_Prophet>

long strands of grass. "Now this is for your muffins, simmer it in water and then add to the mix." Our relationship with Hamish has mutual benefits, he gets fed and I am taught old knowledge. Whenever I am distressed, I bake my way through it, often the fruits of my nerves are so numerous that I take them along to the local pub where my friend and compatriot Marta works. The dogs sit patiently, waiting for the chance to lick up the ends of the mix and a warm fragrant muffin each, for keeping an eye on them so vigilantly!

The milieu of the evening cannot but arrest my attention; the dogs are particularly sweet with each other, nuzzling ears, licking noses and singing little whiney numbers to one another, occasionally looking up to gaze at us adoringly. I notice that William is especially attentive, amorous and expressive. Ladyholm is a picture of calm and domestic harmony – perhaps the fragrant grasses and herbs burning in the front hall have created the ambience? Has Hamish initiated me into witchcraft?!

I stop in to see a lonely Marta. There are enough muffins to go round and I offer them to everyone present, even the 'let's not mention the chickens' neighbour. "You know you have this image in your head of the perfect man?" I notice her accent is picking up the Scottish twang. "Yeah, I never thought mine wouldn't have olive skin and curly black hair!" I reply. "Well exactly, I think it's so funny because you can find yourself suddenly drawn to someone so different"; it occurs to me that she is running her finger around the edge of a glass suspended between the washer and the shelf whilst gazing across the room at the farmer of bear-like proportions. "Oh," I giggle, "shot by Cupid are we?!" She knows I will tease her and turns red, silently resuming her work. It turns out that as a leaving present, Kasia introduced the two after our goats incident and they have been getting on rather well ever since.

It has to be said, 'Love is in the air' in our hamlet! Hamish, the old devil has staged his own version of the film *Chocolat* with Juliette Binoche. She seduces a whole town in her chocolaterie at lent, changing their lives with that old aphrodisiac chocolate. She works her magic and finds love with Johnny Depp – no girl in her right mind would say no to his gypsy charm! We are not quite as beautiful a cast, but the effect is the same; even the 'chickens' neighbour with a shotgun made an offering of some eggs by the front gate. The funny thing is, there is no way Hamish could have seen the film as he doesn't own a television. Perhaps the old devil is secretly working on a book 'Find True Love Between Smoke and Muffins' and we are the test subjects!

For those of you out there who are looking for love, do not despair, say it with a bunch of herbs! Open your hearts and eat any muffins which find their way to you! Happy Valentine's Day!

A Wild Goose Chase for a Book and a Whisky

As Mother's Day draws near, I wonder how I can best celebrate my Mama on this special occasion. Although I am categorically against commercialised 'Hallmark holidays' which have ceased to mean anything besides over-priced cards and flowers, this is a chance for me to honour the woman who inspired and guided me into womanhood. What a gift is a Mother! As a child, she was a mystery of glittering gems, heady perfume and a swish of dresses; undoubtedly the most glamorous and sensual woman I had ever seen. She also had the added accolade of knowing absolutely everything! I turned twenty-five this year and the quarter of a century mark demands special recognition in my life – the girl must eventually become a woman, through decisions and life circumstances, we reach a point of awareness and a way of seeing that we cannot unlearn. However, no one said it was easy.

Mother's Day in our family has a twist as Mama is grateful to my father and I on this day, often giving us flowers or little gifts. Without Dad, she wouldn't have become a mother (at which point he puffs out his chest proudly), and without me, she couldn't practise the art. She always says: "Give me another 100 years and I may become perfect at it." I was always aware that Mama's unconditional love has two conditions: her love may be stretched high and deep, but it must not be abused. The second condition is respect: though my mother is my closest female guide in life, she cannot be treated on the same level as a friend. In response to my very own tribal elder Hamish's question, "Will you be baking one of your specialities?" I answer: "It's a book I'm after, *Women Who Run With the Wolves*; Mama taught me to live in the way the book prescribes."

She inspired me to stand up and fight for my truth if necessary, to listen to and build a relationship with the wild heart within my soul, instead of trying to smother it. Wild women always know 'instinctively when things must die and things must live'; 'they know how to walk away, they know how to stay'.[65] I believe that a strong mother is vital in life, to teach this inner guidance system which must be passed down through the female line. If you are a woman feeling 'fatigued, stressed, frail, depressed, confused, gagged, muzzled, weak, without inspiration, without animation or soulfulness, without meaning, shame-bearing, chronically fuming, volatile, stuck, uncreative,' then you need to awaken the wild within! A healthy woman is "much like a wolf: robust, chock-full, strong life force, life-giving, territorially aware, inventive, loyal, roving."[66]

Hamish scratches his head and begins a 'sermon'; "The value of a gift cannot be measured by its price. The best gifts take the form of attitudes, gestures, sentiments and love. Japan's greatest tea master, Sen no Rikyū established a tradition in which a host invites a friend to his home for a tea ceremony. The room is decorated with

---

65 Clarissa Pinkola Estes, *Women Who Run With The Wolves*, p. 8

66 Ibid p. 12

blossom and an inscription chosen to celebrate their friendship. The tenderness lies in the refinement of the choice and with it, the largeness of the gift it represents." I smile to myself, it is obvious the old devil does more with books than screwing up the pages and loading them onto the fire or pinning them up in my damp hallway! I realise from his recent 'lectures' that he is something of an intellectual. "Do you think you could find this book amongst a quarter of a million of them?!" Hamish snapped me out of my thoughts. "I'd be willing to give it a try," I reply. "Good then, head for Wigtown." I am a woman on a quest once again.

Armed with my trusty sat nav and Hamish's approval, I jump into my red rocket. As I hit Scotland's book town, I am amazed that this sleepy, backward little town, tucked away in a corner of Galloway, was transformed in 1998 into a notorious destination for eccentrics and bibliophiles. I am presented with the largest second-hand bookshop in Scotland and the far from second-hand-charm of its proud proprietor Shaun Bythell.

As I walk around the cavern containing 100,000 books, I think to myself that for some of us, nothing more in life would be needed than a bed and an endless supply of tea amongst the shelves. Like Anne Fadiman, I find that my expectations of new and second-hand book shops are very different. From the new I expect: 'cleanliness, computer monitors and rigorous alphabetisation' and from a second-hand book shop the preference is for 'indifferent house-keeping, sleeping cats' and 'organisational chaos'.[67] George Orwell documented his experience of working as a clerk in a second-hand book shop in his 1936 essay *Bookshop Memories*. He found the reality of long hours in a freezing shop, shelves full of dead flies and dealing with lunatic customers was enough for the books to lose their allure; "I really did love books... the sight and smell and feel of them... as soon as I went to work in the bookshop I stopped buying books. Seen in the mass... books were boring, even slightly sickening."[68] Thankfully,

67 Anne Fadiman, *Ex Libris*, p.123

68 George Orwell's essay *Bookshop Memories*, in *'The Collected Essays, Journalism and Letters of George Orwell'* 1968.

Shaun seems not to have been afflicted by disenchantment and 'The Bookshop' thrives on the energy and enthusiasm we have for old books and the collective knowledge of human experience they represent. Shaun explains the beauty of his work lies in each day being a surprise: "You never know what you're going to get, one morning a £30,000 book might be walked into the shop," in the meantime, it is obviously an enjoyable wait. Book addicts, bird watchers and whisky lovers all flock to Wigtown on the quest for their respective interests – what a combination! For some birds there is only one possible destination – Wigtown Bay, which is how it is for wild geese, wildfowl and ospreys and down the road, Bladnoch Distillery produces a whisky for every palate.

"What's all this fuss about books and reading?" the 15,00 strong population are entitled to ask – "Does it automatically make us wiser and better?" Or the ubiquitous question: "What makes a good book good?!" Without going into a lengthy answer, it is simple: you can live without a book, but you cannot live without a sofa. However, lying on a sofa without a book only faintly resembles life!

I manage to locate a copy of Clarissa Pinkola Estes's *Women Who Run With the Wolves* and escape from the shop, after bidding farewell to 'my friends' and not succumbing to the desire of a quick patrol of the shelves. Something of a bible for the feminine it is a fascinating collection of stories coupled with Freudian analysis and a healthy dose of magic! It is enlightening and empowering for every woman in search of her inner spirit because in every one of us there is a wild and powerful creature, filled with sound instincts, passionate creativity and ageless knowing. Society attempts to 'civilise us into rigid roles without souls. Without Wild Woman, we become over-domesticated, fearful, uncreative and trapped.' I would like to share this jewel of archetypal wisdom with all women on Mother's Day. Mama always used to tell me, "My darling Zosia, if you are lucky in life you will have more than one mother, perhaps many, to get all that you need". There is always hope for those who temperamentally do not fit in with their genetic family as we often choose a whole array of contributors. I would like to wish all my mothers a wonderful Mothering Sunday this year and let's celebrate all women because in a sense, we are all mothers.

Time for a Spring Clean

Spring is officially here; daffodils are blooming in their golden shades and tiny lambs are to be seen frolicking in the fields. This year they are even more irresistible than ever, as many farmers have invested in little plastic jackets which defend against lashings of wind and rain in patches of freak weather in Scotland. The sight of tiny fluffy white balls in their coats, cavorting in the grass, but never too far from Mother Sheep is heart-warming. Despite flash floods and snows, which have made many of us double-check, the vernal equinox did occur on the 21st March and introduced the new season.

Once again, nature resurrects itself, releasing all the pent-up energy of hibernation. It is time for Eastern thinking; each season creates an energy which dictates how we ought to cook, live and harmonise with it. When living in the country, a long and dark winter can make us miss the proximity of others and the hum of city life. However, one sunny day makes it all worthwhile. My teacher at the nutritional school I attended in Glasgow, told us that she was only aware it was spring when she looked down at her plate and saw a reflection of the colours outside her window. Vegetables should start to take over your plates from now on and throughout spring/summer – particularly salads, sprouts and raw food which imbibe that upward, renewing energy, as we migrate away from longer cooked stews and soups.

Snowdrops, daffodils, crocuses and tulips are the first flowers of spring and they are characterised by this powerful rising energy. Symbolising rebirth and new beginnings; the daffodil is said to be the flower of abundance, so go and feast your senses on a walk somewhere they spread their golden light! Don't forget that 10-15 minutes of sunshine is enough to help our bodies produce vitamin D and to make a substantial difference to how we feel, so it is well worth investing in outside time to banish the wintry blues.

The wind picks up and the air is clear as the earth is swept by a refreshing, renewing force. I come out of the house and feel like jumping for joy on my trampoline. The dogs join me (still relishing the absence of the legendary goats). The thrill of the upward force, blowing my hair and shaking my brain around in my head is exhilarating; a perfect opportunity to question the negative thought patterns we allow our minds to spoon-feed us. Things are moving and it is a great time for a detox and a shake-up of the lymph system. Over the cold months we often become more sluggish and our body is quicker to store fats in our reserves. Now is a good time to kick start the metabolism with exercise and diet. Those of us who are church-goers will be participating in the abstinence of Lent; however, whatever your religious persuasion, a customised form of Lent is a good idea for us all health wise. If we abstain from one or more of our favourite indulgences for at least one month, the body has a real chance to flush out toxins and regenerate itself before we start again! The body can only do one thing at a time: it is either protecting or repairing, but we must give it the chance!

Suddenly there is a commotion at the gate and Hamish emerges through a cacophony of barking, pushing a wheelbarrow loaded with a cargo of manure, torturous looking gadgets, shovels, spades and pitchforks. There is no escape I think to myself, contemplating how much lonelier life would seem here without the welcome intrusions of our old friend. It is amazing that in a time when we are diseased by unnatural social propriety, Hamish just barges in and never asks whether or not it is convenient! I have stopped testing the hardness of my skull and the resistance of my bladder on the trampoline as Hamish approaches with his precious brown sack full of seeds. "I'm sure you have already cleaned the house and fasted for forty days," he says and we both laugh out loud. "Now it is time to listen to the awakening earth."

I don't even have time to run inside (and get my still un-used flower print gardening gloves which William bought me) before there is a shovel in my hand and a beautiful polka-dotted seed. "You need to get the mantra going," Hamish tells me, as if I would know what that is… "You know – sow with the flow." Forget cuddly Easter bunnies, forego chocolate eggs and cake. Under Hamish's guidance we dig, prepare the seed beds by raking the ground and strim the grass before mowing it. A job from which I am exempt, having nearly ended up in the field after trying to use William's new mower and strimming the heads off our solar lamps last time! The shrubs are mercilessly pruned, any dead matter is cut back, to reveal plump buds on each stem. We of course don't forget to nourish the soil (not the plants) with pungent manure, which the dogs love to gulp down – straight. Now it's time for the seed to spring forth the new life which has sat so patiently inside it, waiting for soil and water, into action – amazing. Once all the urgent tasks are completed, there is time for a hot-cross bun after all. Rolling my cigarette and burning my mouth on earl grey tea, I feel blissful, having participated in a dance with Gaia, the mythological earth goddess. With just a little effort, I have ensured that I will be privy to a miracle and the soil will offer nutrient-rich tasty gifts.

"I would have liked to have been born in a summer garden," I said to Hamish, smiling as I remember the best reply to the question, "How old are you?" I have ever heard. My Mama did not feel to answer traditionally (as any woman might), so she replied "I was born on a warm summer's afternoon, it was a Wednesday; the birds were singing as the wind ruffled the leaves on the trees." The reply left the person too stunned to speak! I ask Hamish when he was born, whilst happily munching. "It was the year of the Dragon." "That sounds about right!" I exclaim, half choking on the last puff of my cigarette! I know that the equinox is recognised as the start of a new astrological cycle, but I have not been drawn to astrology more than looking up at the evening sky. Hamish began to speak, I could tell it was going to be a lesson by his tone:

"According to legend, the Lord Buddha summoned all the animals of the earth to him before he departed the world. Only twelve made the journey successfully. In gratitude, Buddha rewarded them by naming a year after each one in the twelve year cycle of the Chinese calendar. The system is extremely practical. The Dragon is depicted as a mythical adversary in Western legends, but the Orientals see him as the epitome of style and wisdom. As for you my dear, you were born in the year of the sheep I believe – before you despair, what the Westerner sees as docile and even stupid, the Eastern mind views as sensitive and artistic."

St. Ninian's Cave

This is good news I think to myself, casting my mind back to the conversation I had with a farmer's wife the other day whilst sharing my enthusiasm for the lambs in their red and blue jackets. She said it really only made the slightest bit of difference because sheep are born to die, no matter what precautions you take and even those which are rejected and taken into the barn to be hand-reared only have a 50% chance. I'm definitely sticking with the Eastern view on this one!

"So, Mr Astrologer, what kind of year does this one bode to be?" I inquire. I can tell that Hamish likes this subject, "It is the year of the Tiger; a dramatic year for the world, natural disasters will not be uncommon and the milieu will be volatile – financially it will be a rollercoaster." He becomes very quiet. "Have you any petrol in the red rocket?" I am suddenly asked – "Um, yes, where are we going?" I gulp, what does the crazy, old goat want now I wonder. It is apparently time to visit the Cradle of Christianity in Scotland. We departed on a pilgrimage of sorts, with Hamish as guide to Whithorn which is the nearest town to St.Ninian's Cave.

The cave is a holy site for pilgrimages to celebrate Scotland's first saint, who introduced Christianity to the land. The holy man named Nynia used this quiet and secluded spot as a place for solitude and retreat. He built the first Christian church in Scotland in AD 397, of whitewashed stone, so it could be easily seen. The 'White House' led to the name Whithorn. When I look at Hamish walking in his tattered sandals and overgrown beard towards the tiny cave, accompanied by the roar of rolling waves and angry sky I feel humbled and moved. Far from the religious implications, the natural beauty of the place and its serenity speak a universal language. As we walk back from the beach, Hamish looks at peace with his beliefs, having completed his duties as thousands have before him.

Back home I am rounding up the spiritual harvest of my forty day fast – I did it! There is an old Chinese proverb: when we are born we are assigned a pile of food. When we consume it, we die. Why hurry to the grave then, I ask ? This is a good way to think about your health and the consequences of mindless eating; the concept of mind, body and spirit is not just a conspiracy of enlightened life coaches and therapists. A healthy mind and body result in clearer emotional states to lead you down the right path. I mean, let's not kid ourselves here – we have to make sacrifices – however, I have got my diet on track. As for the rest – prepare for preaching – there is no point in being gorgeous if your life is a mess. End a codependent relationship, quit a dead-end job, and ditch any toxic friends! Smile a lot and give compliments out whenever you have the impulse, remember it comes back three times as powerfully according to karmic law. Get your dream job – people who love what they do are not looking for another person to fulfil them. Search for your dream man if you have not already found him. Adopt the mantra – feel the fear and do it anyway! I leave you to contemplate the wise words of Tsem Tulku Rinpoche : "We keep looking outside for the light when we should now become the light".

A Handful of Ash

Larry the lamb

On the 10th April 2010, a plane carrying Poland's president, his wife and all his political team including the head of the military, top politicians and their families exploded into flames killing all ninety-six on board. The plane crashed whilst trying to land at Russia's Smolensk airport. The visit was in commemoration of the Katyń massacre in 1940 where Stalin's secret police murdered 22,000 Polish military officials. Four days later, on the 14th April, Icelandic volcano Eyjafjallajökull broke through the glacier which bears it's name and propelled a huge tongue of lava, smoke and ash into the air.

A national disaster for Poland and a natural disaster for Europe left the world astounded. We take so much for granted, air travel is pretty close to *Star Trek's* beaming device, taking us anywhere on the globe in a matter of hours. Mother Nature has voiced her dissatisfaction and history has expressed its cruel sense of irony. We have no choice but to be humbled because the first consolation is that there is nobody to blame – volcanoes do not have to answer to us and neither does Majestic History. Planes do fall out of the sky and the air-space above us can be locked. We are completely at the mercy of fate, or the events around us and it seems that the task of living is making the best of the present moment. Never has *carpe diem* seemed truer – we really do not know when we could lose the things which we rely on as the solid, background tapestries of our world. When things are too devastating to take in, there is quietness in the air but the delicate equilibrium of the ecosystem and historical justice have been disturbed.

There are lessons to be learned from both these events. Disasters and tragedies remind us that death is the only certainty in this life. Our constant companion, we fool ourselves in our cushioned, modern life into thinking that we can cheat the Grim Reaper with our medicines and technology, that we can somehow buy time and be more prepared; but the planet has its own ideas. Eventually, the wind will lift the cloud of volcanic ash and the sky will calm; the Polish people will learn how to live with loss and go on, laying new foundations for the future. As Robert F. Kennedy said in 1966, "Like or not, we live in interesting times." The recession coupled with the recent events, acts of terrorism and nuclear weapons status all make for quite a broth.

I have been drawing on Ram Dass of late; "Everything in your life is there as a vehicle for your transformation. Use it!" When we see things from this perspective something interesting happens. Not only are seemingly cruel and random events changed into stumbling blocks to be conquered, they are actually challenges which stretch us and open our hearts. They are markers which show us where we stand in relation to emotional attachment and our need to control. We take so much for granted in our arrogance

– tragedies of the natural and public kind seem to be the only things which make us humble en masse. Carl Jung, the founder of modern psychology, used the word 'synchronicity' to describe random but seemingly related events. Some of us call them coincidences; others prefer the idea that there is a hidden hand which guides and connects all things. Death is a profound teacher. It asks us how long we will allow 'the spoiler' as Barry Long called the mind, to rob us of the riches of this experience on earth?

Suddenly, the 2012 prophecies do not seem a far-fetched fantasy of the doom-mongers. A couple of simultaneous natural disasters like erupting volcanoes could paralyse all air travel indefinitely. Volcanic fall-out could then prevent us from being outside because of pollution – in Scandinavia people with asthma and allergies were told not to leave the house due to the ash. Thousands of people have been grounded for days all over the world, trying to get home – a country's whole political elite were wiped out on a historical remembrance day – suddenly there is a sense of camaraderie and connection as we unite to face this. (Naturally, this applies to the general public only, as travel companies have shamelessly hitched their rates in a desperate attempt to make back some of their losses.)

Experiencing grief allows us to see life more acutely and we learn to connect to the wider world at a deeper level, as Oscar Wilde said; "Pain wears no mask." It encourages us to become lovers of what is happening in any given moment because we have no power to affect it – what can we do but surrender wholeheartedly? The work of Byron Katie has inspired many people in this way of perceiving the world. Her theory is: 'It simply *is*, until it isn't'. It does not sound like rocket science, but when fully realised, this is a real tool for freedom in the present moment. In the end, our need to have answers for things cannot change what has already been. There are reasons which explain and reasons which justify, but at some point, we have to stop searching for a cause. To quote James Baldwin: "People are trapped in history, and history is trapped in them;"[69] for how long must we keep digging before

69 James Baldwin in his essay "Stranger in the Village", first published in

we allow the grace of trust to wash over us? Let us not repeat Pandora's mythical situation. After opening the forbidden box, she allowed horrors man had never experienced out into the world, but Hope was left inside the box. Euripides said human hope and courage enable us to "bear what heaven sends."

It is no wonder that in times like these people turn to God, the Universe or their faith in humanity. When we are thrown from our delusions of grandeur we must bow our heads and wonder suddenly; 'there must be more than this...' Whatever we believe affects our reality directly, so it is worth having a think about what you really turn to when you are deeply touched. People who believe everything to be arbitrary also find their own freedom in using this belief to seize the present moment and enjoy it. So, whatever stories your mind is feeding you, remember that you are the narrator and you can change the script, or simply adapt your interpretation of it.

I have been spending much time at my father's house lately, as my role has become a full-time job. I have ample time for reflection and William and I have the space to miss one another and the excitement of being reunited – something which is so necessary in a relationship (especially once clear of the honey moon period). I have been avidly reading the spiritual seeker's bible – it is called *A Course in Miracles,* and I found that I was nourished in faith after finding this passage: "What could you not accept, if you but knew that everything happens, all events, past, present and to come, are gently planned by One Whose only purpose is your good?"[70] Whether or not one believes this, it is a comfort and new opportunities can present themselves. For example, Poland will have a whole new political elite, perhaps we will change the way we travel and begin to take the ferry which is more natural for body, as it has time to adjust to different climates and time-zones; appreciating the journey more than the destination.

After the recent events, I was in need of a mood enhancer

Harper's Magazine, 1953.

70 Helen Cohn Schucman, *A Course in Miracles,* Lesson 135

which I found at the stables. Larry-the-lamb was rejected by his mother at birth. She had twins and when there is a long gap between the first and the second lamb, the mother often rejects the first born. In cases where the lambs are stillborn, farmers often skin a dead lamb and cover a rejected lamb in its skin. The mother sheep will then accept it as hers and begin to clean it; the skin can then be removed and disposed of. It seems rather bloody and gruesome, but it guarantees survival for the cutest little creatures. Larry was not so lucky and he was left without a mother or a surrogate – the future was bleak – until the ladies at the stables got involved and decided to rescue him. Since then, Larry has been living at the stables with the cat and the horses. He is bottle-fed several times a day after demonstrating his thirst by pulling back his little lips to expose two tiny teeth. Feeding Larry is like having a hit of endorphins! It is magical and I walk down to feed our new friend each day with my brother. Clearly, it is obvious that I am a London girl – people who have grown up in the country have seen so many Larrys that they cease to be a source of boundless curiosity and joy!

There was a national tragedy and a natural disaster which shocked us. Yet a tiny life was saved and it brings causeless joy to all those around it. I am a part of that. What if a life of meaning is as simple as that? Forget grand schemes of saving the world, or even your family, and simply get involved in something which makes your heart brim over with compassion... When one of my father's best friends died a few years ago, we decided to plant a tree for him. We never fail to think of him when we walk past the tree and tend to it. Hamish, Marta, William and I all planted some remembrance trees in the woods where we walk the dogs, to commemorate this event. The act itself brought us closer to each other because we worked towards a higher goal. I hope that we as a people manage to find a way forward which is marked by positive learning and not compounding tragedy. My thoughts go out to all of you.[71]

71 Since the writing of this article in April 2010, there are still many unanswered questions about the accident in Smolensk. It has added to the smarting wound in the Polish psyche which Katyń already was.

Message in a Bottle

When my phone began to buzz and bleep in the middle of the night, I had forgotten that I was on 'duty' – I was sure it was another call from one of my friends who had been having relationship trouble lately. A classic case of low moods and wine induced crying – just what I needed at 5.30 am! I had to re-read the message five times. Slowly, I shrugged myself free of the sleepy arms of Morpheus to arrive in a space of surprise. It was a friend who was going out for a run at this ungodly hour "in gratitude for life." I was impressed – not only did he wake up with a profound thought, he also acted on it.

As a species, one of our quirks, or what I am tempted to call malfunctions, is that we seem to be unable to fully appreciate anything we are blessed with unless it becomes threatened, or we lose it completely. Our best teacher of this is: death. Most people remember everything about the first time in their life that someone was taken from them. How the loss changed their world and how their childhood innocence was somehow never quite the same again; after the finality of death had found its way into thoughts, dreams and nightmares.

I was forced to become conscious of the cracks that had begun to show in this dream world William and I had created. Even our idyllic country life, far from the ills of civilisation, with only our love and our pets as company, was not able to sustain us. I had done such a good job of ignoring this fact that it came as a sudden shock when everything was revealed at once. It seemed as though we were so far up the stream that nothing short of a tsunami would shift our dynamic. A paddle (chat), was not going to get us very far at this stage I thought; because the fear of losing any part of this dream inhibited me from seeing its flaws. I did not want to admit to myself that this – our life together – was not enough as it was.

So began a long few weeks of searching and not finding. I went to the closest thing to home – being so far from Mama, I felt further than ever from my beloved Polska, where my heart sings in connection with the people and the land. My 'mini-Zakopany' in the next town, where Marta is to be found pulling pints of real ale behind the bar was going to have to do. A whisky was under my nose before I had a chance to take off my jacket – clearly my inner landscape was displaying itself on my brow. I tested Wojciech Młynarski's theory I had heard in a ballad once, to look for truth and happiness in the bottom of a glass.

There were many glasses and bottoms of bottles. I called for the gypsy of the ballads, but an Irishman on a flute had to do. My conclusion; drinking is like dancing – we drink either to remember or to forget. Seems like I have been doing both. Many tears later, Hamish just 'happened' to walk into the pub for his nightcap; 'accidentally on purpose' I think to myself, he sits down next to me as if we were strangers. I am sure William has sent him to work out what is consuming my joy of life.

The scene seems completely surreal to me as I stagger home in my high-heeled Belstaff Boots with Hamish padding along in his sandals by my side, along the muddy and meandering path. I am crying, Hamish is singing something under his breath. I do not pay any attention to him, I did not ask for his company and even under the influence of the elixir of truth, I find myself unable to express the cause of my malaise. Hamish directs me to my favourite bench at the foot of the garden. "Listen lassie," he begins, "I know you're having a rough time right now and that's ok, but you need to know what is really going on here," I made no attempt at making this into a conversation. It would be a monologue. Hamish was used to those. Unabashed he continued as the words poured over me like water off a duck's back…

"Happiness is a choice. The only question here is: are you willing to accept your partner completely? If you are able to do this, then you accept yourself one hundred percent and the uncertainty will fade.

You will find the conviction to iron things out as they come up. There is no way however to avoid that which drives you mad about your partner; they will always be themselves. Can you give them and yourself the permission for once, to actually be that which they are?"

He was not getting an answer, the only thing on my mind at this point was the gourmet snack I was going to make myself as soon as I walked in the door... "Think on it lass." As he said the last words, he helped me to my feet and escorted me to the door, before turning on his heel and vanishing into the night.

Marta's attempts at words of wisdom in the vein of "William is a lovely guy but there are plenty of fish in the sea," were not conducive to my current state. I decided to go to my dad's for a few days to try and make sense of the unease which was coming closer to panic and devastation every time I checked my internal thermometer. It was definitely time to face the internal music. Everything I seemed to pick up echoed Hamish's words which I remembered somewhat hazily. Rumi assailed me: "Your task is not to seek for love, but merely to seek and find all the barriers within yourself that you have built against it." I remembered Isabel Allende writing about the notion of expecting someone to give you love wrapped as a gift, and it's impossibility – you have to cultivate it and work on it every day. Somehow the phrases: 'Have fun, life is short' and 'carpe diem' seemed to fall on their faces, empty of value – because actually, life is long – we need a plan! We cannot simply flit like butterflies; a degree of commitment is needed to make anything seem worthwhile. I felt I was catching my breath.

My heart began to speak to me, now that it was quiet enough for me to listen. Gratitude for life seemed like a pretty good place to start – ancient peoples have always worshipped life in all her might as an anecdote to heartache which can become all consuming. A line of communication opened between William and I, it seemed clearer than in the last couple of months. We must have exchanged hundreds of emails and text messages over the past few weeks, some even of poetic value – I giggle as I imagine the collected emails of Lord Byron!

A bluebell field

The Price of Elegance

While having a casual conversation with my London girlfriend Marianna who works for a fashion magazine, we broached an ever present problem – the dwindling budget. I am realising that the cost of being a well-manicured 21st century female is immense: "I never seem to be able to get my hands on my money!" I complain. "Half of it is gone as soon as it comes in, because it is owed and today I'll be hit badly again – it's maintenance day!" My girlfriend is sympathetic as she has to keep up with an impeccable standard at the magazine, her suggestion: "Talk to your boss, give him the figures, its £5,000 per year to be respectable in the office, that's the average." Marianna knows me well enough from our student days to know that unless she backs up her latest fashion update with a book, my concentration span is shorter than a goldfish. "There is this slim, grey volume in a satin cover, entitled *A Guide to Elegance* by Genevieve Antoine Dariaux; her mission in life was to transform a plain woman into an elegant one, clearly she dedicated her life to the likes of you Sophia!" Now I was hooked, the description of the book was intriguing; when I heard 'out of print' in Waterstone's, the bibliophile in me went into rapture!

I am on a pilgrimage again, for the Holy Grail of fashion. I head straight for my version of paradise: Scotland's book town, Wigtown. My obsession with second-hand books is well documented by my friends as a spiritual illness, which cannot be explained to the unafflicted. I carefully pull out the book, causing the dust on the shelf to rise in puffs; it was exactly what Marianna promised. The book oozed charisma and respect, with the title sparkling like a glistening coin surrounded by the intoxicating smell of the mould and mildew inseparable from the unevenly stacked volumes. Elaborate script announces: "Elegance is rare in the modern world, largely because it requires precision, attention to detail, and the careful development of a delicate taste in all forms of manners. It does not come easily to most women and never will." Great, how will it ever come to me?! I think quickly, utilising my IQ of 100-plus (I am not prepared to reveal all my secrets!). If you, like me, may fail here disastrously, then do not panic – there are personal stylists who shop with you and wrap you in flattering fabrics for all occasions, match your hair to your skin tone and makeup; creating a masterpiece!

In the past, housewives or to my mind -'House Queens' – operated in a well-planned week; there was washing day, ironing day and shopping day (for necessities). All these duties have become somewhat haphazard, as three decades later find a day in the monthly planner which may soon appear in Filofaxes: maintenance day! In order to be presentable, at least one solid day per month must be dedicated to keep up with all that is necessary. Hair must be either coloured or styled, nails must be painted, tanning (if you like being orange). Excuse my cynicism but I simply cannot understand why being pale is unfashionable and forms of hair removal must be performed. Exfoliating and moisturising are an essential part of the routine, as well as hundreds of extras such as face masks and hair treatments. I am reminded of a *Sex and the City* episode when Carrie asks her partner: "Do you think I wake up looking this good?" as she points out her well-manicured nails, flawless makeup, styled hair and artfully chosen dress complete with Jimmy Choo heels. Imagine Carrie jumping out of bed without any grooming – scary if you ask me!

Women are constantly bombarded with the 'new' way of doing the same thing in the aggressive language of advertising – "You're worth it!"- until you have handed over your money and then you are condemned to call centre customer services manned by a computer! Make no mistake – maintenance day is the most costly in the monthly planner, when credit cards are red-hot! Just in case you hadn't had enough yet, there is the lower region of the female body, an arena where designers and style opportunists have found a niche to torture us and our purses. They set trends, and open endless, easily accessible beauty parlours to have a 'Brazilian' or a 'Hollywood'. It's just like ordering a coffee in America – a hundred different options – it is a conspiracy against the modern woman!

This is only the actual body itself – now imagine that you have to clothe it! We live under constant pressure to update and accessorise our styles. Even when you have saved for a special garment, instantly, another trend has ousted it from its place. Call me old-fashioned, but I still think that a little black number with a string of single pearls can never look out of place and is always elegant. Drawing on my new-found style bible, it seems that a French woman's wardrobe is not typically enormous, she will however have many accessories in order to remake her outfit each time she wears it. They also rarely deviate from darker colours, remaining within the black to grey spectrum. With less experimentation in bright colours which are difficult to wear, there is less room for mistakes. We are so daring in the UK, embracing every fashion, even when it is completely unsuitable for our climate – regular calamities are inevitable!

I love the fact that in Newton Stewart, the biggest town close to my father's house, women of all ages congregate at 'Claire's', the best hairdresser's and beauticians, for a good 'pick-me-up'. It never fails to be an uplifting experience of endless cups of green tea, head-massage and a drop of red wine on a Friday afternoon, whilst listening to the latest intrigue in the town. Forget the pub – this is the place to be – you can come on your own and not get bothered by sleazy men! Even the most fragile grannies come in for their regular curlers and blue tints, which is a testament to the spirit of women that I so admire – you have to keep making an effort, otherwise we might as well live in tracksuits, slob around on the couch and stuff ourselves with sweeties!

I was raised in constantly changing and fresh spaces, Mama's interior designing meant that we moved often and updated styles regularly. My friends always loved to be in the refreshing amalgamations of gothic, minimalist and traditional styles she created.

I contrast this with my auntie's permanent family home which I adored as a child; the biggest change in all these years has been the colour scheme of the cupboards, I could walk through that the kitchen blindfolded and locate everything. However, in terms of a fertile style ground to inspire fresh creations of the wardrobe and 'the look', I can see why my Mama could not have inhabited a space like this. It does however not liberate her from my dogged insistence (to this day), that the lack of posters or any adornment in my teenage bedrooms was a serious cause of rebellion!

Perhaps I should not be too hard on my cousin and her friends in America. While visiting her last year, I was glued to the bed with my eyes fixed open as she proudly paraded her collection of clothes – which could pay off my student debt and then some – complete with designer tags. By the time she got to the shoes I was in a state of disbelief; even her favourite pair looked as though they had only been for a jaunt round the shop! All this in a student style, shared flat on an unimpressive income; "Do you think I've got the foundations for a decent wardrobe?" she asked me seriously, at the close of the elaborate show. My advice, with a few emphatic expletives, was that she should open a boutique!

I am smiling whilst writing this since I have become a bit of an obsessive dresser! Determined to look sharp in the office, I carefully camouflage the signs of any late nights and over indulgences in wine! I plan my outfits the night before and alternate them with different decoration. I remember sitting in a café in the front row on the Champs Elysées, sipping sugared citron pressé (lemon water) and observing the passing women, all well dressed, exuding confidence and total mastery of their bodies. After all, elegance is a state of mind. As I nurture a fledgling joy in dressing and presenting myself as a grown-up, I realise that I have taken another step on the ladder. The girl becomes a woman and the woman becomes an elegant Goddess – long may it last! I am immersing myself in the meaning of style, fashion and vision for and of women. The story of Coco Chanel is an important lesson on this subject; in breaking the images men and history have imposed on us.

I have so often condemned all these matters as superficial

pursuits; however, if you care for and respect yourself; you want to look your best. I cannot deny that I feel amazing when my hair is freshly coloured and I'm wearing a new dress. Ultimately, I can live with the pain, the cost and the time, because the result is brilliant!

I find myself contemplating fashion as I walk through a meadow of bluebells which are extremely elegant en masse; initially, makeup began because women wanted to emulate the beauty of nature's variety. Incidentally, the bluebell is a symbol of humility, gratitude and everlasting love. Why not say 'Thank you' to existence by wearing a flower in your hair? It's my way of accessorising for spring.

The Bonds of Matrimony

As we enter summer, the glorious sunshine encourages people to tie the knot in inventive ways. I accepted a wonderful invitation recently, accompanying William to a wedding. On a personal note, things between us had been out in the cold. The obvious excuse was simply pragmatic, there was so much for me to do at dad's office that I was spending time away from home. However, I had moved from my previous focus on William and fears about whether he wanted our 'experiment' to continue, into realising that it was me who was not sure. Still in the crux of figuring out if I was ready to pursue this path, plagued by torturous pangs of doubt, desire, heartbreak and optimism, I seized the invitation, although I had no idea what to expect.

It was to be a spiritual ceremony conducted by a Hawaiian shaman and consequently, the question of what to wear was a widespread concern. The weather was scorching in the verdant Derbyshire countryside and several ladies I bumped into at the B&B were eager to discuss outfits. I was sure that the outrageous option would have gone down well, but I decided to stick with a long classic silk dress, cut on a bias, which can never look out of place (thank-you Dariaux!). William looked dashing in a well-cut grey summer suit and we had matching 'favours' which are the Scottish equivalent of a corsage –complete with thistles, tartan ribbon and a white rose for the lady.

Whether we think of marriage as warfare or as a delightful adventure; it belongs to the category of the most dangerous and potentially expensive inventions! Isadora Duncan wrote that "Any woman who reads a marriage contract and then goes into it, deserves all the consequences;" I wonder how she would feel about the cult of the prenuptial agreement?! However, the most entertained dream of the majority of little girls still seems to be their wedding day. It certainly was not mine; I remember telling my Mama at the age of five that I hated boys – she sat down in front of me and said: "Darling, I know that there will come a day when you will not feel that way." This memory often amuses me, as I realise that the anarchist inside me is slowly being eroded, by a more traditional woman who would like to stand against the world with the man of her choice.

The guests were a mix of classic, smart and totally New Age ensembles. The ceremony followed a traditional style at first. The bride and groom both stood under a veranda in their glistening whites, as the first speaker delivered the legally binding: 'for better or for worse, for richer, for poorer, in sickness and in health, to love and to cherish; until death do us part' vows.

It was unbearably hot; people were visibly burning and sheltering their faces under song sheets, when the Hawaiian shaman took the stage in a long-sleeved, embroidered, violet, velvet blazer. He announced that he liked to take a bit of Hawaii with him wherever he went! Suddenly, where we had struggled to hear the words before and sit still with the sweat beads trickling down our faces, it was as though the voltage had been turned up, everyone sat straighter; his voice boomed and held the energy of the clearing where we were seated. Plant spores started to drift down from the sky, creating the surreal effect of a snowstorm in the heat. We recognised his words instinctively as the truth – he talked of the dark nights which are bound to face the couple at some point and about our duty as those gathered to witness their union, to help them in times of need, when the clarity of their decision may be obscured. Tears began to trickle and couples embraced. I sought William's hand and as we locked eyes and exchanged a tender kiss, there was a recognition of the true feeling between us. Although we did not know where we were headed, my heart sang in the knowledge that he was mirroring my experience and being able to share a moment together, completely vulnerable and unplagued by everyday trivialities was a gift.

The blessings of the four elements were invoked and honoured by sharing a little water, earth, lighting a candle and breathing on the couple (by the shaman). Inhaling another's breath is a symbol for sharing the spirit of life; the couple rubbed noses and blew on each other's faces, according to the Hawaiian ritual, which was the greeting amongst all islanders in days gone by. When Captain Cook arrived with his handshake, the white man became known as the "Haole" or those who give no breath ('Ha' is the breath of life and 'Ole' means no or none).[72]

Biblically speaking, God caused Adam to fall into a deep sleep and it took marriage to wake him; a man is incomplete until he is married... Then he is finished! The words of American writer Helen Rowland are the most touching I have read on this subject: "Woman was taken out of man; not out of his head to top him, nor out of his feet to be trampled underfoot; but out of his side to be equal to him, under his arm to be protected, and near his heart to be loved." Unfortunately, marriages are often miserable ghosts of their once romantic, affectionate, mutually supportive relationship-selves. I am in pursuit of a fairy-tale marriage – one that does not end at the close of the wedding party with 'They lived happily ever after'. I have already seen a few couples who have devoted themselves so completely to the big day, that in its passing they have experienced an anti-climax and no longer had much to talk about. The process has also been known to end some marriages before they have even begun.

The preoccupation of our culture with marriage is endless; the institution of wedding planners, dramatised films on the subject of cultural weddings, run away brides, wedding singers, party crashers, wedding dates for hire, drunken marriages in Las Vegas and the wedding blues abound! A sweet story on marriage is that of *Muriel's Wedding*, about the long-harboured desire of an ordinary girl to walk down the altar – it was a success of course.

With at least half of traditional marriages ending in divorce, with spectacular and vulgar exposition of details if you are

---

72 http://www.haskell.edu/red_center/papers/MALAE_KA_LAMAKU.pdf

unfortunate enough to be a celebrity – why do we do it? The first time round we have the excuse of curiosity and naivety but what about the serial offenders? Zsa Zsa Gabor springs to mind, she used to say that she was the perfect housewife because she always kept the houses (after divorce that is) and never hated the man enough to throw the engagement ring back at him! Say you have landed yourself a dream man: he has chased you and presented you with a rock that made Alcatraz blush, the story is just beginning. After weeks of daydreaming, the reality of organising the actual wedding kicks in: the hen night, the dress, the venue – church or registry office? Should you exchange vows in the open air – in the park, cruising the Thames or go further afield? Then there is the guest-list, the date, the flowers, the hair, the cake, the bridesmaids, the music, the first dance, the honeymoon and then – the bill, it is like taking a dip in sub-zero water! The reality is that this is only the beginning, if you survived it, well done, now begins the rest of your life; you must become a wonderful spouse.

According to Peter de Vries, the American novelist, "The bonds of matrimony are like any other bonds – they mature slowly," which leads us back to the crux of the issue – those who imagine that marriage is the solution will have a rude awakening! The old Polish tradition of 'bramy' or obstacles recognises the partnership necessary in the face of life's challenges. If we, as the shaman said, keep stepping towards our partner with love each day, our hearts will be opened and we will grow within the most rewarding union possible.

If you, like me, find the 'til death do us part' vows a little heavy handed, there are a multitude of interesting strands which can be incorporated into a declaration of commitment. Neale Donald Walsch designed a new marriage contract, in which the couples vow to support the other for their highest spiritual development: unconditionally. The beauty of this is the introduction of selflessness, of supporting and loving the other, however life unfolds. With the current statistics of the traditional approach, spiritual ceremonies may be the way forward. I know that I would like a mix of cultural elements, some of my favourites are the Druid incantation:

"We swear by peace and love to stand/ Heart to heart and hand to hand." The Celtic version of 'til death do us part,' which I much prefer: "I will cherish and honour you through this life and into the next" and a vow from a spiritual ceremony: "I choose you as the soul with whom I will spend the rest of this life, I am honoured to tell those present and the whole world, every living creature." A note of sweetness and sensuality from the Celts: "I pledge to you that yours will be the name I cry aloud in the night and the eyes into which I smile in the morning." Another source of inspiration are couples who renew their vows every year – naturally, this would be a private affair, bringing into consciousness the intent of standing together regularly. We all crave a 'happy ending' and know at least one couple who inspire us; there is no reason why we cannot rebel against the statistics and invent new ways of making a commitment to the one we love. Whether we choose to do it with a pledge of some kind, an almighty party, or simply by sharing the way together, I think everyone resonates with Rumi: "May this marriage be full of laughter, our everyday in paradise."

Fatherly Love

I recently stumbled upon an old story book of mine, which contained an entry written for Father's Day. As I read the scrawl and the copious amounts of red ink from the teacher's pen, I remembered it was around this time that Dad became my hero. Erich Fromm writes that generally, children up to the point of eight years old, are concerned with 'being loved for what one is': from this age on, for the first time, the impulse of *giving* something to the mother or father arises. The child suddenly becomes conscious of 'creating love', as another of its mediums of relating to the outer world. This phase is invaluable in the creation of big-hearted adults, who know 'the potency of producing love by loving', because, the more you love, the more you become a magnet for love in your world.

People hardly ever seem to ask dads how they cope with the stresses of fatherhood, careers and marriage. This strikes me as a little unfair, although I do not doubt that women have a more draining time with lack of sleep, loss of identity for several years and the hormonal and physical changes which go with the territory. However, fathers are expected to 'cope' with not being vital to the child for the first few years. The bond with the mother is incredibly strong and the new-born learns her every movement: she *is* survival. My dad taught me that a man's job is to make a safe environment for the woman, for the first couple of years and to protect her from as many of the strains of life (bills, cleaning, mortgages) as possible, so that she can fully be there with the child. It is only when the child 'learns to walk, talk and explore the world on his own; the relationship to mother loses some of its vital significance and the relationship to father becomes more and more important'. Many relationships do not make it through the first few of years of childrearing and I wonder how much of this is due to a lack of education on the subject. I think any man would be happy and proud in his role as home protector, if he understood that his partner's sudden shift of attention would soon come full-circle, as the child begins to look from 'the home' which is mother, to father; 'who teaches the child' and 'shows him the road into the world' (Fromm).

My dad's qualities as I saw them then were: muscles, kindness, strictness, a sense of fun and being silly (a highly attuned sense of the ridiculous is one of things I appreciate most about my Dad to this day). 'He plays with Mummy' (in the form of pillow fighting contests); a vital component of harmonious family life – everyone ought to cultivate their playfulness; not just the children. I distinctly remember there being talk of money problems and I could not understand it; I thought Dad along with all men, went to a factory where he made the money himself at a machine. If anyone needed more, I thought they could simply stay at the machine longer! I am sure Dad appreciated my humour when I proudly read him the story on Father's Day – the description of his eating with his mouth open must have been softened by the qualifying statement: 'I like his eating habits'! There were fantastic yachting trips, explorations of Florida and brilliant expeditions to the 'Sweet Factory' for enormous 'gob stoppers' and bags brimming with 'pick n' mix'! My five-year-old self's conclusion on the subject of Daddy is that 'He loves me and he loves Mummy too', which summed it up for five-year-old Zosia and for twenty-five year old Zosia!

The missing part of the story is the essence of paternal presence later in your life, manifesting in guidance and wisdom. 'Anyone can be a father, but it takes someone special to be a dad' (Anon); never have those words been truer, in our times of sperm banks, surrogates and IVF clinics. Amongst my friends, family is a subject which always seems to present itself after a few drinks. I used to think it was such a misunderstanding in my teenage years, when my friends and I were arguing with 'the parents', that they imagined we left the house and forgot about the situation by having fun. This was not the case. When someone had a bad time at home, they were always burdened with troubles – not joy riding or kissing in the cinema! Similarly, if we think that *because* we are adults; we have dealt with our family issues, it is usually a misconception. We never 'get over it' all completely, because the early years colour our character fundamentally. When I look back, I can see the wisdom in the message my Dad imparted to me: "Live your truth without unnecessarily hurting another" and his prescience, in trusting that I would learn my lessons myself. As many a parent of John Ciardi's 'unreturned prodigal', Dad kept 'his house open to hope' without judgement. Of course, I could not have lived without my Mama, but Dad helped me to sculpt myself into the person I wanted to become. One of the most important lessons, reinforced by both my parents (from observation), was a healthy dose of rebellion and how to use it to stand my own ground. Naturally, through adolescence, neither of my them believed that I was expressing something from our family system, but I had a genetic double dose!

I phoned around my friends, intrigued, with the question: 'How important has your father's presence been in your life?' Invariably, answers started slowly, people said things like, "It's difficult to say..." before delivering reports which were profound. Even if, as Nietzsche writes, "One has not had a good father, one must create one" whether this is in the shape of one person in your life, or an amalgamation of many. Alice Walker touched my heart when I read this: "It no longer bothers me that I may be constantly searching for father figures; by this time, I have found several and dearly enjoyed knowing them all;" for me this encapsulates the experience of being a child with several bonus-parents!

It is clear that a staple lesson taught at parental school is that of 'the disappointed look'. It must be highlighted as the bonus of living through the terrible twos and the rough waters of adolescence – 'Once an adult stands in front of you; you can play this hand!' Parental disapproval is somehow more effective when delivered from fathers. Good old dads have few emotional foibles and leave the teary issues to their female counterparts, while they dish out the components of our consciences!

Almost every woman must have experienced something of the over-protective father or brother who is indifferent, bordering on disapproving of her choice of boyfriend. This causes a severe conflict in the psyche. I can imagine Freud sitting behind the proverbial couch, pronouncing the verdict: 'Oedipus never sleeps!.' We all know the theory, but somehow, we do not register that it is natural for a five-year-old to find that no one is as amazing as their Daddy! He is the strongest, bravest and most magnificent person in the world. If you are a little boy, you want to become him and win someone as lovely as your Mummy, and as a little girl, you wish to meet someone just like Daddy. As we grow, our eyes (hopefully) flutter open and we begin to hit maturity when we can see our parents as people in their own right, without idolising or vilifying them. In short, we have grown up when we treat our parents like children!

The mother and father within are important motions within our psyche. Do not fret if your biological parents leave much to be desired, or simply have never been there – we assimilate the energies we need from other people in our lives and from those, we fashion our own internal guidance systems. The question really is – what is your frame of reference? What are the paradigms of character and worth which you value? We can glean much about our internal motivations and often unconscious belief systems through these questions.

Blesséd be the uncles, grandfathers, older brothers, teachers, social workers and friends who provide us with the guidance so necessary for our development. I once read that it would take nine fully enlightened individuals to meet a child's needs; for those of us who have not been so lucky, we can be grateful for the patchwork of paternal faces who people our world. Without them, we would sorely struggle to function in the world of: 'thought, of man-made things, law and order, of discipline, of travel and adventure' (Fromm). I can happily go forward in life, safe in the knowledge that 'He (my Daddy) loves me'! A heartfelt 'Thank-you' to my fantastic Dad and all those who take the task of guiding youth into flowering as morally autonomous human beings seriously.

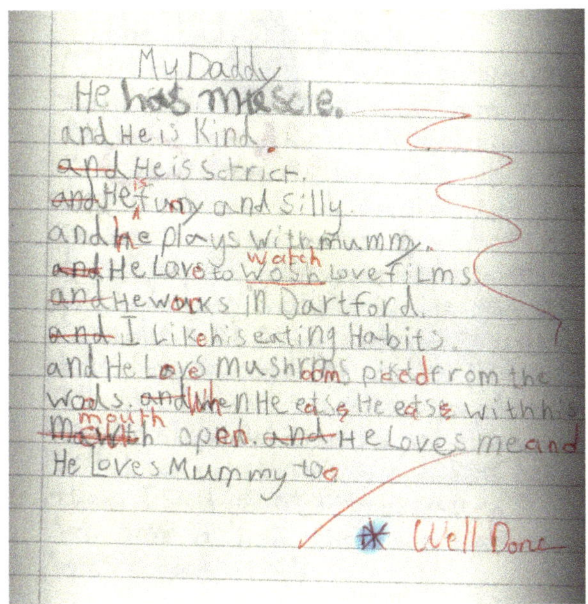

My Daddy

He has muscle.
and He is Kind.
and He is strict.
and He funy and silly.
and he plays with mummy.
and He Love to wosh lovefilms
and He works in Dartford.
and I Like his eating Habits.
and He Loves mushrooms piked from the
woods. and when He eatse He eatse with his
mouth open. and He Loves me and
He Loves Mummy too

Well Done

A New Chapter

The time between August and September is known the 'Indian summer'. It actually originated in the USA and was a term which crept into prairie farmers' lexicon. It is often mistakenly thought to have originated in the days of the British colonisation of India. It is the transitional time from the light and warmth of the summer, into the rusty colours and sounds of autumn; when the energy of intensity begins to settle. A certain pause takes place when we stop to feel it. This sweet and mellow time of year ushers in the harvest.

In love, passion recedes into introspection; it is a time for addressing and assimilating the sometimes flashing tempers of summer and highly charged emotions in relationships. As the conkers drop to the ground, life feels a little more serious than in the heat and we tend towards nostalgia and a touch of melancholia as the evenings draw in and the colourful carpet of leaves weans us from the bright days into the bleaker mornings to come.

After eating macrobiotically for just six months, you start responding to natural rhythms. They guide you like a compass, as moods and cravings calm themselves. The whole grains and vegetables hold you on an even keel, not often rocked by urgent cravings for sugar or comfort foods. I find myself living according to the law of attraction and repulsion with regards to 'rubbish' thoughts and words, phrases and associations which we are constantly accumulating (mostly unconsciously). I can hear my inner voice in the quiet times now; she tells me that when I start skidding, I must steer in the direction in which I am pushed, only this way is eventual equilibrium regained.

After a two year wait, Ania's wedding finally arrived and our

'Snob Club' reassembled in Kraków. Our little conglomerate; a mixture of pure bloods and mongrels, all living in the Polish diaspora could not wait to meet up again. Kraków came to each us the first time as a stop gap: we were reluctant to completely relinquish studentdom and begin 'serious' life. I was curious to see how we had all moved on.

I was pleased to see that some things do not change; our favourite barman and dear friend Maciek served us our remembered favourites in '*Wódka*' (vodka) bar. We had to recognise that each of us was adrift in the world and once again, the homeland brought out the spark we needed to return to our lives with renewed gusto; for soulless jobs to be left, dissertations to be written and serious plans to be laid.

The wedding was a wonderful fusion of traditions and cultures; the Italians were not sure what to do with the rice (our version of confetti), how to handle the Polish vodka which was flowing ceaselessly from open buckets and the meaning of the *bramy*' positively baffled them. In the spirit of the 2010 South African Fifa World Cup; vuvuzelas were pulled from the Italian cars during the negotiations to allow the bride and groom to pass!

At some point during the reception, the language barriers began to fade away. When we shouted "*Gorzko! Gorzko*!" – meaning 'bitter' – the bride and groom had to kiss to sweeten the atmosphere, and as the kisses became more and more passionate, the guests howled with delight. At which point the men on the groom's side put a shoe in their mouths and began a tango of sorts amongst themselves. We are still unsure whether this is a custom, or simply the effect of our Wyborowa vodka!

Living together in Kraków as a family would be a brilliant prospect for The Snobs! We struck up a deal: if in time to come we find ourselves isolated and lonely, we will all return and open a bar together. A contingency plan made in heaven! Even if it never comes to pass, the thought itself cushions the harsher blows of life in which we learn the lessons we need, to become who we are to be.

A new chapter begins now for Ania as Mrs Esposito, and for William and I: new paths. The miraculous alchemy of transforming

William and me into 'us' didn't happen and we separated like oil and water. In relationships we find out more about ourselves than we care to know. So why do we bother to engage in them?! Yes, for the obvious; sharing, companionship and beating everyday challenges together. But on a deeper level the purpose of relationships is to learn how to love. Love isn't just for the lucky ones, it's for those who are willing to learn.

In times of acute distress, I always find myself reaching out for philosophies which put things into perspective. The urgency of despair drives us to the brink of madness and sometimes beyond. How can we love fiercely and passionately and be expected to 'get over it', 'move on' and 'accept it' when we don't want to?! It is an incomprehensible business. It is difficult to know when to fight and when to accept; does surrender mean inaction? How can we act when we cannot trust our instincts, because they are so coloured by our emotional drive? Can we ever come back from hurting each other deeply?

By all accounts, this seems to be a ripe time for spiritual development. There is something about the depth of agony and pain which activates the immediateness of life; colours look more distinct, everything tastes sharper, every conversation you engage in feels divinely inspired; gleaning untold pearls of wisdom. For those of you who, like me are experiencing this state, intermingled with a total trust in the universal order, the consolation is that many people have become enlightened in these situations! The great mystic Osho would instruct couples who had parted to kneel at one another's feet, expressing gratitude for the opportunity of coming into contact with their own pain, provided by the other (something which never comes into our minds to do before the coffin is nailed shut).

I feel that our general approach to ending relationships in our civilisation is comparable to war. Both sides are hurt in different ways and suffering heavy losses; there can be no winners. I know that a day will come on our planet, when people will leave relationships peacefully, lovingly and respectfully. According to Neale Donald Walsh, this will take the form of the 'As you wish' and the 'I want for you what you want for you' ethos which will govern all human relationships as we continue our spiritual and emotional evolution.

I grow tired of being suspended between healing and growth: thoughts and impulses battle one another as I sit, surrendering all to the universe. On miserable days, when positive thinking would get a kick in the posterior, I think back to something I once heard: each soul has agreed to this life, to learn the lessons offered. Many times, it is the people who are the closest to us, the ones with whom we have shared many lives, who agree to teach us the toughest lessons. When the dark night of the soul comes calling and the tears fall faster than the leaves from the autumn trees, this belief helps me. Perhaps it is worth examining any 'enemies' we have declared in our lives, people we have condemned. A reversal of this process is fundamental to the completion of it: we must also let ourselves off the guilt-hook with compassion, for any wrongs we have committed. In the eyes of the soul, there is only love – sometimes it is misguided – but each person will be reduced to this vibration again, until we are pulled into the next adventure!

Forgiveness happens. It is a spontaneous combustion, not something which can be rushed into or consciously attained. I comfort myself with the knowledge that if something is meant to be, it will be and that everything happens according to the divine plan. We never lose when we love because wisdom and tenderness only grow when we tend to our inner landscapes. In the words of Randy Pausch, a man who knew he was dying when he gave his TED lecture, "Experience is what you get when you don't get what you want." Even when all cheerfulness abandons me, nature's declining and resurgent cycles are a source of hope, even for a bruised heart like mine. One thing is certain; we must always have the energy, no matter how poor the harvest, to sow the seeds of hope once again. I find myself gently leaning on Scarlett O'Hara's "Tomorrow is another day."

As the house returned to bricks and mortar, slowly emptied of our memories; of the goats who ate our vegetable plot, of the exceedingly numerous potato yield, the ordeal of finding Caine the bachelor some company; Hamish appeared bearing pomegranates. We sat with the ruby juice rolling down our chins in silence, as though time didn't matter, whilst I desire with all my being that memory, the most subjective editor who retouches the past, will leave me only the sunny days. The old goat never fails to disappoint and I only realise the full impact of his last 'teaching' when I am in solitude. "You know my dear." he begins, with a coy smile which quickly fades as his eyes sweep over the meadows, "There is not one person who has truly lived, who would wish to be young again. It would be hellish, to repeat all one's lessons, to experience the insecurities of youth! It becomes obvious that there can be no regrets, because we have done what we can with the resources available to us at the time." He sighs and smiles. With those words, he turns on his heel and like a Cherokee Indian, leaves without a goodbye.

Instinctively we always know when it's time to leave, even if we don't have a particular place to go.

The Snob club at Ania's Wedding

After the End

Dear Reader,

If you're still reading, I hope you enjoyed the journey.

I know that I will never come back here and even if I do, it will not be a return, just a visit. I shall carry the landscape of Scotland with me forever.

Although I'm in the region of the doldrums now, I shall be watching the sky and the weather with reasonable interest. I will go where the wind blows, believing in T.S. Eliot's words: "What we **call** the beginning is often the end. And to make an end is to make a beginning. The end is where we start from".

Until then,
Sophia Wasiak Butler.

PS. As for Hamish, I know we will meet again.

CPSIA information can be obtained
at www.ICGtesting.com
Printed in the USA
BVHW020441080819
555308BV00021BA/1300/P